Great Railway Eras

Festiniog
in the Sixties

Vic Mitchell and Allan Garraway

MP Middleton Press

Cover picture: *Merddin Emrys* arrives at Harbour Station with the 4.30pm from Tan-y-bwlch on 21st July 1961, the locomotive running without a cab in the early 1960s. The points seen under the train were repositioned in 1967 to lengthen the carriage sidings. (A.G.W.Garraway)

To our loyal supporters :
Moyra Garraway
Barbara Mitchell

Published April 1997

ISBN 1 873793 91 X

© Middleton Press 1997

Design - Deborah Goodridge

Published by Middleton Press
Easebourne Lane
Midhurst
West Sussex
GU29 9AZ
Tel: 01730 813169
Fax: 01730 812601

Printed & bound by Biddles Ltd,
Guildford and Kings Lynn

CONTENTS

PASSENGER JOURNEYS

1960	102,032
1961	109,112
1962	114,027
1963	128,543
1964	144,047
1965	150,502
1966	173,789
1967	220,834
1968	294,151
1969	319,327

INDEX TO FR LOCATIONS

Pictures included mainly for their technical interest are not listed.

(J.C.Gillham)

ACKNOWLEDGEMENTS

Our appreciation of the photographic contributions to this album goes to John Alexander, John Andrews and Norman Gurley. Thankfully Arthur Lambert and Michael Seymour have helped by checking the facts. All have also worked tirelessly for the FR for many decades! Thanks to David and Susan Salter for proof reading. The *FR Chronology* masterminded by Jim Hewett has been most helpful.

The map in the 1960 FR Guide Book did not divulge the fact that nearly half the railway was still closed. Services were "temporarily suspended", an important legal point. An Act of Parliament would have been required for closure. If it had been closed, the land could have reverted to the neighbouring landowners.

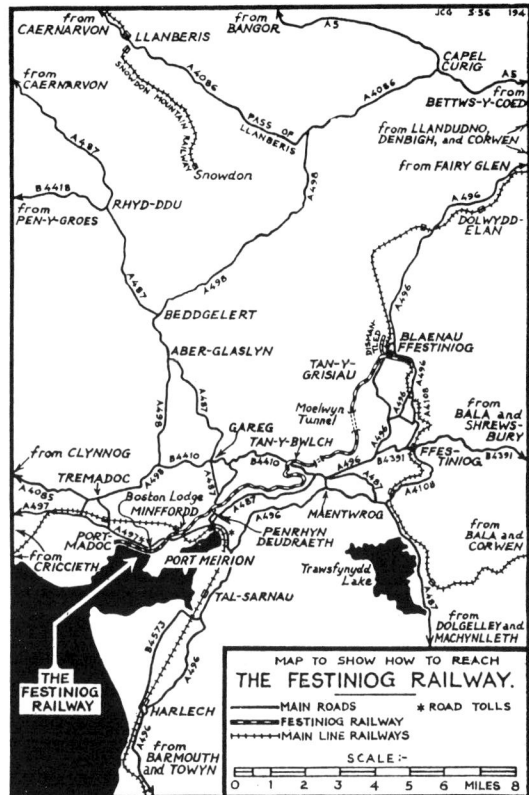

MAP TO SHOW HOW TO REACH
THE FESTINIOG RAILWAY.

INTRODUCTION

In this album we assume that the reader has some knowledge of the geography of the Festiniog Railway, why it had only one "F" instead of two and an understanding of its great historical importance in the development of narrow gauge railways worldwide. For those wishing to know more of these aspects of the line, there are many other publications including albums from Middleton Press entitled *Branch Lines around Portmadoc 1923-46, Branch Lines around Porthmadog 1954-94* and *Porthmadog to Blaenau*.

This book comes as the result of the success of our *Festiniog in the Fifties*. Throughout the 1960s and for more than another decade, Allan Garraway was general manager and for much of the period was also driver of *Linda*. In the early sixties, Vic Mitchell was a director of the Festiniog Railway Society Ltd and a volunteer in many departments of the railway.

In many ways, the 1960s was the most dramatic period in the revival of the Festiniog Railway. The half-way point had been reached in 1958 with the reopening of the line to Tan-y-bwlch but the challenge of keeping a thoroughly worn out railway operational was enormous. There were no wealthy benefactors and little in the way of grants. Volunteers had tedious and slow journeys to reach the FR and some were attracted away by new and more varied railway revival schemes nearer to their homes.

The year 1962 was the most critical and one in which the entire resuscitation process could have suffered a grievous setback had not *Linda* been available for hire from the Penrhyn Railway, and had not staff and volunteers been prepared to work most of the night on many occasions.

Flooding of part of the top half of the line by the Pumped Storage Scheme lower lake had been anticipated in the 1950s but it was not until 1960 that the Lands Tribunal published its disappointing decision regarding compensation payment for reinstatement. The subsequent 16-year long legal battle is now case history but little time was lost in commencing the Deviation. The work can only be touched upon in this album, which is intended to focus upon the difficulties and successes of the functional railway.

A number of operating innovations were employed in the early sixties such as a non-stop train at 3.00pm from Portmadoc. This ran only at peak times.

Unlike the other Middleton Press albums on the FR in which the photographs are in geographical sequence, the illustrations herein are mostly in chronological order. Additional background information can be found in part of *Garraway Father and Son* (Middleton Press). Other views of some of the events pictured in this publication can be seen in *Branch Lines around Porthmadog 1954-94* and *Porthmadog to Blaenau* by referring to the relevant location.

During the first half of the era, Allan Garraway contributed a NEWS FROM PORTMADOC column in the quarterly Festiniog Railway Magazine. These are reproduced herein, slightly abridged, and with the complex punctuation then still in fashion, to create the atmosphere of the times. In the second half of the era, this became NEWS FROM THE LINE, which was a team effort and has had to receive greater pruning. This title is used throughout. The paragraphs appeared some time after the events and are similarly positioned herein.

The achievements of the staff and volunteers in this period were monumental and were made because the FR had a unique and very important place in railway history. All were conscious of the need for the line to continue to evolve and progress, but its special position should never be forgotten and rival schemes must never eclipse it.

Allan Garraway - Boat of Garten
Vic Mitchell - Midhurst
March 1997

FESTINIOG RAILWAY - 1961 - TIMETABLE

		EASTER 31 Mar.–8 Apl. WEDS. ONLY 12 Apl.–17 May WHIT S'DAY 21 May 25 - 30 Sept. WEDS. ONLY 4 & 11 October	SPRING AND AUTUMN SERVICE 20 May — 8 July 11 Sept. — 23 Sept. WEEKDAYS ONLY	SUMMER SERVICE 9 JULY—10 SEPTEMBER MONDAY TO FRIDAY						SATURDAY			SUN.
							3		T.W.Th.				
Portmadoc (Harbour)	dep.	2·30	10·45 2·30 4·30	10·30	12·30	2·30	2·45	4·30	7·30	10·45	2·30 4·30	2·30
Pen Cob (Halt)	,,	dd	dd dd dd	dd	—	—	—	dd	—	dd	dd dd	—
Boston Lodge (Halt)	,,	dd	dd dd dd	dd	dd	ee	dd	dd	dd	dd	dd dd	—
Minffordd (for B.R.(W))	,,	2·42	10·57 2·42 4·44	10·42	12·40	ee	2·58	4·44	dd	10·57	2·42 4·42	2·42
Pen-y-Bryn (Halt)	,,	dd	dd dd dd	dd	—	—	dd	dd	dd	dd	dd dd	dd
Penrhyn	,,	2·48	11·03 2·48 4·48	10·48	dd	ee	3·08	4·48	dd	11·03	2·48 4·48	2·48
Tan-y-Bwlch	arr.	3·15	11·30 3·15 5·15	11·15	1·10	3·08	3·31	5·15	8·10	11·30	3·15 5·15	3·15
Dduallt		Service temporarily suspended											
Tan-y-Grisiau													
Blaenau Ffestiniog			Tan-y-Bwlch ...... dep. 1·25 3·15 Blaenau Ffestiniog (B.R. Sta.) arr. 1·56 3·46	Connections by Crosville Motor Services								
Blaenau Ffestiniog		Service temporarily suspended	Blaenau Ffestiniog (B.R. Sta.) dep. 12·15 2·30 Tan-y-Bwlch ...... arr. 12·46 3·01									
Tan-y-Grisiau													
Dduallt								3		T.W.Th.			
Tan-y-Bwlch	dep.	3·45	11·45 3·30 5·30	11·30	1·25	3·30	4·07	5·30	8·40	11·45	3·30 5·30	3·45
Penrhyn	,,	4·12	12·12 3·57 5·57	11·57	dd	3·57	4·34	5·57	dd	12·12	3·57 5·57	4·12
Pen-y-Bryn (Halt)	,,	dd	dd dd dd	dd	dd	dd	dd	dd	—	dd	dd dd	dd
Minffordd (for B.R.(W))	,,	4·18	12·18 4·03 6·03	12·03	1·55	4·03	4n43	6·03	dd	12·18	4·03 6·03	4·18
Boston Lodge (Halt)	,,	dd	dd dd dd	dd	dd	dd	dd	dd	dd	dd	dd dd	dd
Pen Cob (Halt)	,,	dd	dd dd dd	dd	dd	dd	dd	dd	—	dd	dd dd	dd
Portmadoc (Harbour)	arr.	4·30	12·30 4·15 6·15	12·15	2·05	4·15	4·55	6·15	9·20	12·30	4·15 6·15	4·30

(Spring and Autumn service note: Runs 22–26 May & 27 June – 8 July 11 – 15 Sept. only)

3—Third class only.
n—Arrives 3 mins. earlier.
T.W.Th.—Tues., Wed., Thurs. only

dd—Calls when required to set down on notice to the guard. Passengers wishing to join must give a hand signal to the driver.
ee—From 10 to 21 July, will stop if required.

Harbour Station, Portmadoc.   Telephone:—Portmadoc 2340.

T. STEPHENSON & SONS LTD., PRESCOT, LANCS.

TIME-TABLE 6th APRIL to 27th OCTOBER, 1968

	SPRING			SUMMER			AUTUMN			LATE AUTUMN
	Daily 6 - 26 April Weds. Sats. & Suns. 28 April – 15 May	18 MAY - 20 JULY		21 JULY - 6 SEPTEMBER			7 SEPTEMBER - 15 SEPTEMBER			Daily 16 Sept. to 6 October
		MONDAY—FRIDAY	Saturdays & Sundays	MONDAY—FRIDAY		Saturdays & Sundays	MONDAY—FRIDAY	Saturdays & Sundays		Then every Sat. & Sun. to 27 Oct. also Wednesdays 9 & 16 Oct.
	S&SU X		WO		FX FX			S&SU X		S&SU X
RTMADOC (lft)	1100 1430	1040 11·30 1415 15·05 1635 1945	1130 1415 1635	1000 1040 1130 1225 1320 1415 1505 1600 1650 1745 1945		1130 1415 1505 1635	1040 1130 1415 1505 1635	1130 1415 1635		1100 1430
STON LODGE (lft)	RQ RQ	RQ RQ RQ RQ RQ RQ	RQ RQ RQ	RQ RQ RQ RQ RQ RQ RQ RQ RQ RQ RQ		RQ RQ RQ RQ	RQ RQ RQ RQ RQ	RQ RQ RQ		RQ RQ
NFFORDD (lft)	1109 1439	1049 11·39 1424 15·14 1644 1954	1139 1424 1644	1009 1049 1139 1234 1329 1424 1514 1609 1659 1754 1954		1139 1424 1514 1644	1049 1139 1424 1514 1644	1139 1424 1644		1109 1439
NRHYN (Halt)	1110 1440	1050 11·42 1426 15·16 1647 1956	1142 1426 1647	1010 1050 1142 1237 1331 1426 1516 1611 1703 1756 1956		1142 1426 1516 1647	1050 1142 1426 1516 1647	1142 1426 1647		1110 1440
N·Y·BWLCH (lft)	1135 1505	1115 12·07 1451 15·41 1712 2021	1207 1451 1712	1035 1115 1207 1302 1356 1451 1544 1636 1728 1821 2021		1207 1451 1546 1712	1115 1207 1451 1541 1712	1207 1451 1712		1135 1505
UALLT *	1140 1510	1120 12·12 1456 15·46 1717 2026	1212 1456 1717	1040 1120 1212 1307 1401 1456 1548 1641 1733 1826 2026		1212 1456 1546 1717	1120 1212 1456 1546 1717	1212 1456 1717		1140 1510
N·Y·GRISIAU										
FFESTINIOG	1155 1525	1130 12·22 1506 15·56 1727 2036	1222 1506 1727	1050 1130 1222 1317 1411 1506 1558 1651 1743 1836 2036		1222 1506 1556 1727	1130 1222 1506 1556 1727	1222 1506 1727		1150 1520

| FFESTINIOG | Train services temporarily suspended | Commencing 17 June. Mon.–Fri. only Connections by Crosville Motors Blaenau Ffestiniog . dep. 12 20 Connects with 13 05 Tan-y-Bwlch - - arr. 12 51 dep. from Tan-y-Bwlch Tan-y-Bwlch - - dep. 12 07 Blaenau Ffestiniog - arr. 13 23 arr. at Tan-y-Bwlch | | Mondays — Fridays only CONNECTIONS BY CROSVILLE MOTOR SERVICES Blaenau Ffestiniog . dep. 12 20 Connects with 13 05 Tan-y-Bwlch . . . . arr. 12 51 dep. from Tan-y-Bwlch Tan-y-Bwlch . . . . dep. 12 07 Connects with 12 07 Blaenau Ffestiniog . arr. 13 23 arr. at Tan-y-Bwlch | | | Train services temporarily suspended | Whilst everything possible will be made to ensure running as Time-table, the Festiniog Railway will not guarantee advertised connections in the event of breakdown or other obstruction of services. | | |
| N·Y·GRISIAU | | | | | | | | | | |

	S&SU X				FX				S&SU X		S&SU X
UALLT *	ZZ	ZZ	1156 12·45 1530 16·01 1740 2044	1245 1530 1740	1115 1206 1245 1335 1440 1530 1620 1715 1810 1844 2044		1245 1530 1610 1740	1245 1530 1740		1200 1535
N·Y·BWLCH (lft)	ZZ	ZZ	1206 12·55 1540 16·20 1750 2058	1255 1540 1750	1113 1206 1245 1335 1435 1540 1630 1725 1820 1854 2054		1255 1540 1621 1750	1255 1540 1750		1201 1545
NRHYN (Halt)	1220 1550	1211 13·05 1545 16·21 1751 2055	1305 1545 1751	1116 1211 1305 1400 1453 1545 1637 1730 1822 1855 2055		1305 1545 1621 1751	1305 1545 1751		1211 1546
NFFORDD (lft)	1245 1615	1236 13·30 1610 16·46 1816 2120	1330 1610 1816	1141 1236 1330 1425 1518 1610 1702 1755 1847 1920 2120		1330 1610 1646 1816	1330 1610 1816		1236 1611
STON LODGE (lft)	1247 1617	1238 13·32 1612 16·48 1817 2121	1332 1612 1817	1143 1238 1332 1427 1520 1612 1704 1757 1848 1921 2121		1332 1612 1648 1817	1332 1612 1817		1237 1612
RTMADOC (lft)	1256 1626	1247 13·41 1621 16·57 1826 2130	1341 1621 1826	1152 1247 1341 1436 1529 1621 1713 1806 1857 1930 2130		1341 1621 1657 1826	1341 1621 1826		1246 1621

To assist punctuality at busy times the booking office will close 5 minutes before departure time

—Commences 3rd June.
—Train does not run during the full period of the Time-table.
Q—Calls to take up or set down on request. To board, passengers should give hand signal to the driver. To alight, please give notice to the guard on boarding.
FX—Fridays excepted.
S&SU X—Saturdays and Sundays excepted.
*—There is NO road access to Dduallt Station. Access by foot is over very rough and ill-defined footpaths suitable only for appropriately equipped walkers.
Z—From 6 April until 15 May, owing to major engineering work, there will be no passenger facilities at Dduallt station and passengers will not be able to alight. Trains will return immediately to Tan-y-Bwlch where standing time will be allowed.
WO—Wednesdays only.

PRINCIPAL FARES

	Return		Single	
	1st	3rd	1st	3rd
Portmadoc to Dduallt ...	14/-	9/-		
Portmadoc to Tan-y-Bwlch	12/-	7/-	7/-	4/-

Special Fare: Portmadoc to Dduallt returning to Tan-y-Bwlch (or vice versa) 7/- 3rd Class.   10/- 1st Class.
Children under 14 half price; Under 3 free.

Down trains leave Penrhyn Halt approximately twenty minutes after leaving Tan-y-Bwlch. Up trains approximately five minutes after leaving Minffordd.

Down trains leave Boston Lodge Halt approximately four minutes after leaving Minffordd. Up trains leave approximately five minutes after departing from Portmadoc.

Trains also stop at Plas Halt and Campbell's Platform on request.

OBSERVATION AND BUFFET CARS ON ALL TRAINS   1st & 3rd CLASS

Over the Easter holiday this time-table is subject to alteration. At other times additional trains may be run. (See local announcements)

Special parties by arrangement. Please apply to the General Manager, Festiniog Railway Company, Portmadoc, Caernarvonshire, North Wales

TELEPHONE: PORTMADOC 2340

Published by the Festiniog Railway Company, Portmadoc, Caerns., and printed by T Stephenson & Sons Ltd., Prescot, Lancs

1960

NEWS FROM THE LINE - Winter 1960

After such a beautiful summer, it is hardly surprising that the autumn has been correspondingly wet—fortunately from some points of view, as a serious water shortage developed and the danger of lineside fires was acute.

The most striking development, readily apparent to anyone approaching Portmadoc from the south and east, is the extensive work at Rhiw Plas. A new road overbridge is being built here in connection with the road-widening scheme, and whilst construction is in progress, a temporary level crossing is being prepared. The track has been relaid with check-rails, telephone wires taken underground, and the ditch carried in open-jointed drains. A large quantity of spoil has been dug out, and much of it has been loaded into F.R. wagons and transported to Tan-y-Bwlch to fill the hole beside the road bridge. *Taliesin* has been used for this duty.

The weather has also brought down telephone wires, a tree at Pen Plas, and the weak wall above Rhiw Plas; the latter would have come down to make way for the new bridge in any case.

At Tan-y-Bwlch, the culvert has been strengthened, and concrete pipes laid on the upstream side, surrounded by concrete. Fill (ex-B.R. spent ballast and material from Rhiw Plas) is now being dumped on top, but many hundred tons will be required before it is banked right up.

At Portmadoc Harbour, the former gents' lavatories have been demolished and sundry repairs (chiefly re-flooring) carried out.

At Boston Lodge, work is proceeding slowly on *Merddin Emrys*. Certain repairs have had to be done to the top bogie, and the boiler and its cradle are being prepared for the fitting of the tanks.

Prince has been stripped so as to patch a crack under the valve chest and to fit new side rod brasses.

The wheel-drop has been completed, and all the trackwork refitted and tidied up. The roof has been temporarily supported and new brick piers are now being built to provide permanent support for the roof and overhead gantry.

1. A melancholy view faced General Manager Garraway in February as he looked from Harbour station towards Boston Lodge Works in a severe south-westerly gale. He was the sole occupant of the premises at that time. Salt spray and sand blown into the Works hampered restoration efforts. (A.G.W.Garraway)

2. The turf of the 1950s had given way to fairly smart permanent way. A new doorway on the back of the building meant that passengers could enter from that side for the first time and that the gate in the fence could be locked. The nearest room served as the Ladies. (A.G.W.Garraway)

3. Access to the station building had always been from the platform but 1960 was going to be the first year in which the new double doors on the left would enable passengers to go direct to the booking office and shop. Neither the car park, the station premises nor the track on the Cob were on ground owned by the FR. Thus many problems came about, particularly when planning consent was given for dwellings to be built on the wharves in the mid-1960s. (A.G.W.Garraway)

4. Rhiw Plas bridge, where the main road crosses the FR, was narrow and with sharp turns, inadequate for modern traffic and incapable of carrying the heavy loads being brought in by sea to Portmadoc for the new nuclear power station at Trawsfynydd. Whilst it was being rebuilt a temporary level crossing and road were put in. The first car and Crosville bus to use the new route were recorded on 7th January. (A.G.W.Garraway)

5. The old bridge at Rhiw Plas is seen partially demolished. The surplus stone and materials from the old bridge area were loaded into wagons and taken up to Tan-y-bwlch. The load sometimes justified the use of a double engine. (A.G.W.Garraway)

6. A few of the stone walls supporting the railway showed signs of movement. The one below Tan-y-bwlch road bridge had a "Blister" appear which had to be temporarily strengthened by a flying buttress. The culvert was extended with concrete pipes and the material from Rhiw Plas tipped on top. See picture 83 in *Festiniog in the Fifties*. (A.G.W.Garraway)

NEWS FROM THE LINE
Spring 1960

Throughout the winter, routine maintenance work has proceeded on all three locomotives, as well as on rolling stock and permanent way. The p.w. programme has been somewhat upset, however, by the roadworks at Rhiw Plas, mentioned in our last issue. The temporary level crossing there has now been completed, and our photographs show two views of the new temporary road arrangements.

The restoration of the booking hall at Portmadoc Harbour Station is also progressing satisfactorily, and it is hoped that the new layout, providing a new entrance door in the north wall, will facilitate the handling of passengers, particularly during the rush period in August. It is proposed that they will enter the booking hall via this new door, and pass thence direct to the platform. The interior of the booking hall is being completely modernised.

7. *Taliesin* passes over the temporary level crossing with an Easter down train. The new retaining wall can be seen near the rear coaches. (A.G.W.Garraway)

NEWS FROM THE LINE - Summer 1960

Easter weekend saw the re-opening of the line to passenger traffic for the 1960 season, and the numbers carried show an increase of rather more than thirty per cent over Easter, 1959. Traffic has been well maintained during the pre-Whitsun period, and the increase in the numbers of coach tours which include the F.R. in their itinerary should be reflected in the total figures this season.

The new bridge at Rhiw Plas has been completed and is open to road traffic; the widening of the main road between there and Boston Lodge tollgate is now virtually completed.

The modernized booking office at Harbour Station is in full use, and the new layout has greatly facilitated the handling of passengers, the small gate in the white station fence now being kept locked. On the long wall of the station building facing the town, bold individual letters, painted cream, display:

FESTINIOG RAILWAY HARBOUR STATION.

Much general maintenance work has been carried out on both locomotives and rolling stock, and there has been a general process of tidying up in Boston Lodge Works.

Progress on *Merddin Emrys* has been somewhat slow due to other, more pressing, requirements, but lagging of the boiler is now in hand and the top bogie motion has been reassembled.

Members visiting Portmadoc will, we feel sure, be impressed by the great improvement in appearance of the whole undertaking.

8.   Volunteers were travelling in the six-wheeled Cleminson wagon as *Moelwyn* was recorded at Tan-y-bwlch on 15th April after recovering worn rails. Also evident is spot resleepering at a rail joint, a common practice in the early days of "turf and prayer". (A.G.W.Garraway)

9.   The same train was photographed a short while later as it stood near the southern portal of Moelwyn Tunnel. There is evidence on the right of the rope-worked balanced incline that was in use before the tunnel was completed in 1842. The route of the deviation to the new tunnel obliterated part of this evidence. (A.G.W.Garraway)

10.   Another train was recorded at the same location on 1st May. This special was hauled by *Prince* and was for the pleasure of Tarmac personnel who had worked on the building of the new Rhiw Plas bridge. (A.G.W.Garraway)

11. Chaos still reigned in the old Joiners Shop as a gate, some station lamps and coach no. 16 awaited repair. The restoration of the coach started in 1962 and was completed in July 1978.
(J.L.Alexander)

13. South of the Works, Glan-y-Mor Yard had been partially cleared but *Palmerston* was largely hidden by bushes. In the distance is the roof of one of the disused gunpowder stores, built remote from habitation for safety reasons. (J.L.Alexander)

12. The Blacksmiths Shop was still in "as abandoned" condition with countless valuable components awaiting reuse. The forge is behind the sandpots and the stack of Hudson carriage side panels.
(J.L.Alexander)

14. *Prince's* driving wheel showed signs of movement on the axle; it was also found to have a crack between the axle and the crankpin. Vulcan Foundry came to the rescue by making a new axle and wheels. They were building locos with frames burnt out from slab; the scrap pieces from the lightening holes were just the right size to make new wheel centres. It would appear that pre-war staff had pressed the wheels on too tight; Vulcans had to use 90 tons to get the good one off the axle!
(A.G.W.Garraway)

15. On 13th July BBC TV did a show live from the railway. One camera was mounted on a flat wagon ahead of *Prince*, while all the equipment was in no. 22; behind was another flat with a diesel generator and an aerial array which had to be orientated to the base station on South Snowdon Wharf. From there the signal was relayed to another mobile one on the top of Snowdon, which directed it to their permanent base. Once *Prince* was wired into the train he could not get to water at Portmadoc! (A.G.W.Garraway)

16. Whilst the mobile transmitter went from Highgate Crossing to Cei Mawr, radio signals could not get through, so there were scenes and interviews at Boston Lodge. Tan-y-bwlch was another dead spot, so an interview with Bessie Jones had to be pre-recorded on film. What viewers did not know was that a cow jumped over a wall at Pencefn in front of the 4.30 up train but *Taliesin* was stopped just before a bloody encounter.
(A.G.W.Garraway)

17. The publicity effect of the TV show was tremendous, with traffic breaking all records; the year ended 33% up on 1959. To help handle the crowds every effort was made to get no. 15 (right) usable. It first appeared on 9th August on the "Flea", going back to Boston Lodge each night for more work to be done. It was in grey primer with a full set of seats but without windows by mid-August. On one occasion in this hectic period, a coach wheel dropped inside the track but fortunately rerailed itself. (A.G.W.Garraway)

NEWS FROM THE LINE - Autumn 1960

The most exciting news from Portmadoc is the tremendous amount of traffic carried. On a period-by-period basis, the early part of the season was slightly up on last year's figures, but as Easter and Whitsun were late there were two full weeks of traffic to catch up on, and consequently it was not until July that it could be seen that we really were doing better than last year. Then, on 13th July, took place the finest bit of publicity the line has ever had, when the B.B.C. produced a half-hour's live television broadcast, and from then onwards traffic figures just soared higher and higher.

In 1959, we were very elated when one day we carried 1,000 passenger bookings; this year the record has been broken three times, on 2nd July 1,108, on 11th August 1,203 and a final climax on 30th August of 1,256. On a total of seven days the bookings have been over 1,000, and one week included three individual thousands, and produced a total of 5,700 bookings, 10,302 journeys. These figures do not include the many passengers on inclusive through bookings with B.R., Crosville buses, etc., which last year amounted to 4,500 journeys, and the number of passengers and the number of different tours has greatly increased this year.

Up to 10th September, totals of just on 90,000 journeys and 50,000 bookings have been reached, so that by the end of the season a grand total of about 100,000 journeys should be easily attained when all through booking figures have been included.

Carrying this vast number of people has not been without its difficulties. The 2-30 train throughout August has been filled to capacity every day, Monday to Friday, and the others have been well loaded. Eight-coach trains have been run on many occasions; both the 10-45 and the 4-30 have run with this number several times, and the lunchtime 12-40 has normally been loaded to seven.

The 2-30 has been run up non-stop to Tan-y-Bwlch to allow longer time for run round and for the relief to get away from Penrhyn earlier, thus avoiding too much delay to the 3-30 down. The traffic to intermediate stations has therefore been dealt with by the relief, although on many days both trains were so full that fresh passengers could only get on if some of the people already aboard alighted.

One or two peculiar operating efforts were made. On one occasion the 4-10 left so many passengers behind at Tan-y-Bwlch, and the 4-30 from Portmadoc (with eight coaches) started out so full, that it was realised that all of them could not be carried back by the 5-30 from Tan-y-Bwlch, especially as about fifty were known to be joining from B.R. at Minffordd. When all the B.R. passengers got onto the train the coaches were really groaning under the load (twelve people were counted in one compartment!). An additional train was therefore put on, leaving Portmadoc at 5-30 and crossing at Penrhyn; and it was good to note that sufficient late passengers were freshly booked to pay for the train's coal, etc., whilst the thirty-odd people it picked up at Tan-y-Bwlch were grateful for the additional train, rather than annoyed at being kept waiting.

On another occasion, a large party booked returns to Minffordd on the 4-30, and it was realised that the 4-10 down would be too full to accommodate the entire number. So these passengers were shepherded into the front coach of the 4-30 and, at Minffordd, whilst the B.R. passengers were being loaded on to the up train, this front coach was shunted into the loop and on to the back of the down 4-10—the first through coach working on the F.R. for many years.

All this heavy traffic has, of course, taken its toll, and the track in particular has given some considerable anxiety. Many of the old sleepers, especially on the upper stretches, have just given out under the strain. Will Jones now has an additional mate, however, and they have done a magnificent job in patching up the track to keep the trains running. Probably few people, other than those who have worked the p.w., realise quite how poor some of this track is, and if such heavy traffic is to be worked again in 1961, a tremendous amount of work must be put in this winter. Fortunately, the increased receipts will go a long way to allowing more £ s. d. to be spent on the track, but every possible volunteer will be wanted to assist in preparing the way for Will Jones and his gang to get in hundreds of new sleepers.

Just after Whitsun the track spread on the loop at Tan-y-Bwlch, and *Taliesin* dropped in. The 3-30 down was delayed whilst *Moelwyn* came up, and the 4-30 ran very late, with only a handful of passengers. The re-laying at Tan-y-Bwlch has now been completed—greatly assisted by the parties of lads from the Vulcan Foundry, who are now working on Creua Bank above the station.

During the busy season, most of the p.w. volunteer labour has been utilised in re-laying on several places in the various yards in which the track had become so bad that it was unusable. Much of the curve down into Minffordd yard has been re-laid, and the sunken coal road has been completely cleared out. In Glan-y-Mor yard, re-laying is in progress and slight re-alignment of the sidings is taking place, ready for the rebuilding of the carriage shed which will have to be done to accommodate the additional coaches as they are repaired. This is a long term project which will most likely be left during the winter (so that work can be concentrated on the main line) and resumed next summer.

1961

NEWS FROM THE LINE - Winter 1961

Many people have commented favourably on the increased space alloted to News from Portmadoc in the last magazine. In the autumn, however, with the end of the summer season, there is a lot which can be written on this aspect, whereas in the winter, work continues at a steady pace on maintenance, but does not make a lot of news. Nevertheless, as it has become apparent that some members of the Society are a little confused by the note of warning sounded in Roy Cunningham's letter printed in the same issue as the news of such a successful season, we are devoting a fair amount of space in this issue to a review of the whole situation.

We can now look back with great relief that we got through the season and carried over 102,000 passenger journeys safely. It is that word "safety" however, which is the key, and we just cannot afford to take risks. Early in the season it became obvious that certain sections of the track were deteriorating badly, and Will Jones was finding more unsatisfactory places than he could cope with by patching up. There was not sufficient time to put in new sleepers, and the temporary expedient of shifting the chairs on to the better parts of the sleepers had to be adopted. When sleepers are old and rotten this method is only of limited value.

As soon as the Directors were advised of the position they authorized the engagement of an additional platelayer, and gave instruction that if there was any doubt as to the safety of the track the train services were to be cut short or reduced. If this course had to have been taken it would have had very serious repercussions on our whole future, not only from a prestige standpoint, but also in that revenue would have suffered, and without the revenue less could have been spent on wages and improvements this winter, thus in turn reflecting on the amount of traffic which we should be able to carry in 1961.

Great credit is due to Will Jones and his mate, "Evy" Roberts, who jumped from place to place keeping things safe. (Roberts is another old F.R. platelayer, and consequently well experienced in the work.)

Although the lower half of the line does not contain such poor track as the top section, it had to be closely watched nevertheless. During the early years track was relaid using the minimum amount of new material, and whenever possible the old sleepers were left. This policy got us going, but all those old sleepers are now showing their age and the spikes are not holding properly. Paul Dukes and his gang found some unpleasantly slack places developing, but as they appeared more gradually he was able to put in new sleepers and to do the job thoroughly.

In view of the imperative need for so much work on the main line, it may be wondered why so much has been done in some of the yards. However, in the summer time when train services are heavy, it is very difficult to replace sleepers, and it is obviously inconvenient to do much digging out unless the rubbish can be deposited on the spot. It is consequently more feasible to employ volunteers away from the main line, and they are therefore put on to the yards, which badly need attention, and where the tracks can be completely removed and relaid properly. The yard tracks were completely devoid of effective sleepers, and derailments were so frequent in some places that it became virtually impossible to use a few of the sidings. Derailments waste time, apart from causing damage to vehicles and permanent way, for apart from the people engaged in the re-railing, others are also held up.

This summer, therefore, a start was made in Glan-y-Mor yard, the two lines to the shed and their attendant pointwork having been relaid with standard double head material. The other two lines to the demolished shed will be tackled next summer. At Minffordd, the curve down to the yard, as well as the top points and sundry other spots, have also been relaid.

This winter Will Jones is concentrating on some of the cuttings and curves which are almost impossible to tackle during summer services. The curve below Llechwedd Coed has been relaid, and now the cutting at Penrhediad and up through to Crossing Bothy is being attended to. Quite a lot has also been done between Tylers Curve and Private Station. At the lower end, Paul Dukes and Ron Lester have

been joined by Dai Edwards (from Minffordd Crossing). After finishing off through Boston Lodge Halt and relaying Boston Lodge yard points (the old loco shed), they are working up past the cemetery.

After Christmas, when some large parties from Cambridge and Manchester were at work, the whole p.w. department is combining to relay right through the curves from Sheepfold, via Cutting Gwlyb, to Brynmawr—a very wet stretch with sleepers hard on the rocks. Some good working parties have helped to get the track dug out so that relaying can proceed apace, but of course, there is always room for more help.

Once again may we make a plea for as many volunteers for p.w. work as possible to come in the early part of the season when train services are not too busy, so that the track may be put into a state about which we shall not have too much anxiety. (Whatever work you are going to do, please do not forget to advise Mr. Garraway in advance so that he may plan accordingly.)

Permanent way is the foundation of a railway, and as such must have first priority, but there is a similar story in the other departments. For too long our neighbours have been clamouring to get the gates and fences repaired. They have, in fact, been very patient, but in view of our splendid season of success, think that their problems should now be attended to. Several new gates were made and erected last winter, and Tom Williams, our handyman, assisted by Bill Hoole, is busily at work on more this winter, as well as on repairing fences. Not only is this helping our relationships with our neighbours, but it will also assist in avoiding the delays from sheep being on the line.

As far as the engines are concerned, *Taliesin* does not require much attention, but *Prince* has to be fitted with new cylinders as well as being due for her five-yearly boiler examination. The cylinders are out and away with our good friend, Mr. John Wilkins, who is not only casting and machining the new ones for us, but is doing it without charge to the railway. We are extremely grateful for this generosity. When these cylinders come back there will be quite a lot of work entailed in fitting them to the engine, as well as in replacing the lagging, tanks, cab, etc.

Meanwhile, *Merddin Emrys* makes slow, if not very visible, progress. The time is now approaching, however, when the parts should start being assembled, and then progress will appear more rapid.

The carriages are possibly the biggest problem after the permanent way. We need more coaches, but also we have to keep the present ones going. As with the track, some of the earlier-repaired coaches were tackled as quickly and as simply as possible, and a lot of panels, particularly on the "sunny" sea side, are badly cracked. Apart from visible defects, the timber which carries one of the bogie centres on No. 18 needs replacing. (Although iron is used for the main framework it is timber which actually carries the bogie centre.) No. 15 is now finished, and varnished externally, and Fred Boughey and his stalwarts are resolutely plodding through the coaches, one by one. It is unlikely that they will be able to start upon any new coach work for some time to come. In connection with coaching repairs, many new droplights are required. Some people are busy making these at home, and if there is anyone else who could assist would they please write to Portmadoc.

Had we been able to repair engines, coaches and permanent way properly in the first place it would have taken a little longer then but far less time than the total now being expended. However, had that been the case, we should probably only now be thinking of opening even to Tan-y-Bwlch, and of course, as we should have been running less trains we should not have had the income to spend on so much now. It is hoped that this will explain a little why the Company will not try to progress beyond Tan-y-Bwlch for a while; when there are three engines in first-class order, as well as nine bogies and four 4-wheelers, not forgetting the all important 7¼ miles of track all thoroughly overhauled, we shall be able to put a great deal of our resources into re-opening further stretches.

18. The petrol engine in Simplex, even after conversion to run on TVO, was expensive to operate. In view of the age of the engine, a Gardner 4LK diesel was acquired and fitted in its place. It went for its first run on 14th April, although lacking essential creature comforts. (A.G.W.Garraway)

19. The arrival of the second pair of Hudson bogie wagons from Smiths Crisps Lincolnshire railways was photographed on 19th March. The three smaller ones were used for coal, but the larger one became no. 63 and was provided with a through vacuum pipe so that it could run in passenger trains and be used for all manner of stores movements and other purposes. (A.G.W.Garraway)

20. The operation of a two-train service in 1960 with only two steam locomotives caused much anxiety and burning of the midnight oil. Great effort was made to have *Merddin Emrys* ready for the 1961 season; this was its condition in March. (A.G.W.Garraway)

NEWS FROM THE LINE - Spring 1961

Work after Christmas was concentrated on the Cutting Gwlyb area, and the large working parties at New Year and subsequent weekends enabled the combined p.w. gangs to relay the complete stretch from the staff halt at the bottom of Bryn Mawr down to the bottom end of Sheepfold Curve. Not only has this length been re-sleepered, but all the joints closed up to a more reasonable amount, (this was commenced below Private Station, and by the bottom of Sheepfold Curve a gap of 3ft. had been made). This closing up of joints is being done throughout the line as opportunity allows; the extra length is usually made up where there is a sub-standard rail, by substituting a longer one. The whole stretch through Cutting Gwlyb has been well ballasted so as to lift the track off the rock, and should give a greatly improved ride. Work is continuing downwards from Sheepfold Curve, and the bottom gang are again carrying on their work in the Minffordd—Rhiw Plas area.

Mechanically, work continues on *Merddin Emrys* and the new fabricated cradles have been fitted, and the frames and boiler re-united and prepared for the fitting of new tanks. Meanwhile, the two power bogies have been thoroughly cleaned up; the top one has had quite a lot of work done on the suspension and expansion links, new piston rings, stuffing boxes, etc. *Prince* is slowly being reduced to smaller and smaller components ready for re-staying parts of the firebox, and fitting new cylinders.

No. 20 has been in the shop and has had all the remaining principal mahogany panels replaced by the usual waterproof ply ones, and has had several other minor details attended to.

No. 20 wagon has returned from Birmingham, and although this can hardly be classed as a rebuild as it has been sent back with some of the old ironwork being used, it now has good outside axleboxes and proper spring buffers. It makes a very useful addition to the fleet of small wagons, and it went into service for carrying ballast the day it was completed. The Company is very grateful for this excellent and practical piece of "homework".

The S. & T. section have at last got the E.T.S. into full working order between Minffordd and Portmadoc, complete with intermediate instrument at Boston Lodge, and remote operator at Minffordd for use when the booking office is not manned.

21. The FR coaches rolled like a ship in a rough sea. They also developed lists to one side or the other, but it was impossible to check any of the springs without lifting the coach off the bogies and dismantling the spring gear. Often springs were found broken in several places. The primary springing above the axleboxes was by a nest of short springs in a box but the body sat on a ball and socket pivot, with springs hidden in pots inside the bogie frames and within the carriage cross-members, ostensibly

to keep the coach level. There was no secondary suspension whatsoever. No. 18's bogie was rebuilt utilising available springs. The secondary suspension, being now outside the bogie frames, gave wider support. Hydraulic dampers were fitted and the entire centre casting was bored out so that the coach sat on the springs. These secondary suspension units were pre-fabricated away from the railway by one of the volunteers and all coaches were modified, a single spring above the axlebox being adopted for primary suspension. (A.G.W.Garraway)

22.   Ever on the look-out for useful rolling stock going cheap, cattle truck no. 38089, seen here at Castle Caereinion, was bought from BR in June, but it had to be regauged. Rebuilt by the East Anglian Group in 1964-68, it became FR van no. 9. (A.G.W.Garraway)

23.   The one surviving serviceable quarrymen's coach (it had been under cover in the Joiners Shop) was restored as something to carry a few passengers and also as a braked vehicle to run with the little 4-wheelers, which had no brakes. It was photographed in July and became coach no. 8. (A.G.W.Garraway)

Possibly the most interesting event of these last few months was the emergence of *Merddin Emrys*. After a great struggle by the loco. staff, she went out under her own steam during the evening of Friday, 21st April.

It had been hoped to use *Merddin Emrys* to work the second train on the day of the A.G.M., but as she was still very much untried this was felt to be a little risky; furthermore, she was without vacuum brake. All the nine bogie coaches were therefore assembled together and *Merddin Emrys* was used to assist the re-christened *Earl of Merioneth* from Minffordd to Tan-y-Bwlch.

The cab is so badly moth-eaten that it is obviously best to re-build it, especially as it needs to be modified to go round the new tanks, but the mechanical lubricators, vacuum brake, and proper drawgear are almost fitted.

A second train on the A.G.M. day—consisting of the four-wheelers—was hauled by "modern" power, *Moelwyn* and the dieselized *Simplex*. The latter's conversion is still not complete, but she is proving an extremely useful second diesel. On the down journeys from Tan-y-Bwlch. the *Earl of Merioneth* brought the nine coaches, and *Merddin Emrys* came down with the "modern" power, *Moelwyn* providing vacuum.

The *Earl of Merioneth* has valiantly worked the whole service this season, with no serious trouble. After some of the difficulties last August with being short of steam, other types of coal have been tried out, but unfortunately the Coal Board is unable to supply best Yorkshire steam coal, and have, instead, let us have Derbyshire coal. This proved to be very dirty and smoky and made a lot of ash, causing some delays with heavy trains during Whit week. However, its problems were overcome, but South Wales coal is again being used. This time it's Ogilvie coal, a less viable one than the Devi or Navigation types previously used, and it is giving excellent results. This is

the coal that the Vale of Rheidol abandoned in favour of Yorkshire coal, but our Fairlies seem to like it and have rarely steamed so well.

No. 18 has been in shops for the replacement of the member carrying one end of the bogie. Although these coaches have iron underframes, the bogie centre and bolsters are mounted on an oak member sandwiched between two cross girders, and in this case the weight of the coach was really only taken by eight through bolts, one of which was badly split. The replacement is a fabricated steel member, and, at the same time, the bolster springs are being put outside the bogie frame and fitted with shock absorbers, as on No. 26, in an endeavour to reduce the rolling of these coaches.

On the permanent way, much work has been done on Bryn Mawr and around Minffordd, whilst at Tro Bagl and through to Whistling Curve the track is at present being re-sleepered, and the thin outside rails exchanged with those inside. At Minffordd Crossing, a long welded rail of about fifty feet has been made up to obviate the joint in the roadway.

Ballasting is also being done, and recently a large consignment of twelve B.R. wagons has made for much ballast train working. This work will largely cease now, however, until train services ease in September.

Traffic receipts have been very encouraging. Easter was, of course, a fortnight earlier than last year, but traffic up to the end of Whit week was slightly up on the period to the end of Whit week last year. Up to 10th June there were nearly 13,000 journeys as compared with 9,000 to last 12th June (bearing in mind the two weeks less last year). These two extra weeks of this season have given our figures a nice boost at the outset, and furthermore, the figures are better than might be imagined because none of the pre-booked coach parties are included in this year's weekly totals.

24. *Merddin Emrys* hauled its first passenger train under the new management on 21st July 1961. A view from the footplate soon after includes "Tadpoles", schoolboys from Enfield who undertook valiant clearance work for many years, guided by their teacher Keith Catchpole. (A.G.W.Garraway)

25. Most of the Works had rotten and dangerous timber flooring mounted on joists on slate slabs. A start was made in 1961 to remove it and provide a solid concrete replacement. The first area so treated was the Machine Shop. (J.F.Andrews)

26. The concrete was mixed in the Works Yard in the mobile mixer and laid by volunteers under the professional supervision of Fred Boughey. The cement was stored in a former gunpowder wagon, left. (J.L.Alexander)

27. With the increasing traffic, it made sense to use the passing loop at Penrhyn and run two trains of similar length. Taliesin is seen entering the bottom end of Penrhyn Loop, in August. The photographer is on *Merddin Emrys*. (A.G.W.Garraway)

NEWS FROM THE LINE - Autumn 1961

At this time of year, an item uppermost in everyone's mind is traffic receipts.

Up to the end of August, the number of bookings has been virtually the same as last year, although financially things are quite a bit better. This is accounted for partly by the increase in fares since last August and partly by the slight alteration in accountancy with the coach firms. At the end of June and in early July traffic figures were greatly up on last year, but they have, unfortunately, been down since then. Of course, this may be due to the fact that last year's television programme on 13th July gave a tremendous boost to the second part of the season, but it seems that all holiday areas have reported a very bad slump in business this year at the end of July and early August.

We have had far more traffic from coach firms this season, and during August the trains have been extremely crowded. However, the final figure will be approximately 110,000 passenger journeys.

An additional train was put on at the commencement of the Summer Service, duplicating the 10-30 a.m.; the main portion leaving at 10-20 a.m. followed by the relief at 10-40 a.m. The relief then came down at 12-15 p.m., crossing the 12-30 p.m. up train at Penrhyn, the later departure from Tan-y-Bwlch being necessitated by new coach tours from Llandudno, etc., which were arranged after the original timetable had gone to print.

The two Fairlies were then required to maintain the service, and when the afternoon *Flea* started, the engines shared the work between them, *Merddin Emrys* usually taking the 10-40 a.m., the non-stop 2-30 p.m. and the 4-30 p.m., whilst the *Earl of Merioneth* worked the 10-20 a.m., the 2-45 p.m. and, when running, the 7-30 p.m.

There have been a few slight delays, largely due to varying qualities of coal causing lack of steam, but on two occasions serious mechanical failures took place which delayed the 12-30 p.m., and the *Flea* stock was used for the 2-30 p.m. which crossed the down 1-25 p.m. (running late) at Minffordd. On the second occasion, the 12-30 p.m. had only five coaches, so the afternoon non-stop 2-30 p.m. consisted of eleven vehicles in all, namely Nos. 23, 17, 26, 22, 6, 5, 4, 3, 8 (the re-fitted quarrymen's coach), 2 and 1, in that order.

Due to the illness of his daughter, Fred Boughey was unable to get to Portmadoc between mid-June and August, and the prospect looked very bleak as regards completing the carriage programme in time for the August traffic. All the four-wheelers needed attention, but the permanent staff and several stalwart volunteers managed, not only to complete the strengthening of the underneaths of these coaches, but also to re-build the quarrymen's coach. Large quantities of plywood, well glued and screwed, have enabled this vehicle to take its place in the *Flea*, and so ease the accommodation problem. No. 6, the open vehicle, has been fitted with full-length doors, one from each of ex-Nos. 11 and 12. When the panels were removed, the bars were exposed on which drop lights used to fall. There were two drop lights on either side of the door, and Mr. Boyd's volume I illustrates one of these vehicles (p. 37) and a drawing appears on page 164. When and why these closed vehicles were re-built as opens, and given the decorative panels above the opening as with the original open four-wheelers, remains a mystery.

No. 1 van has been piped for vacuum and fitted with a cock for guard's emergency use, and No. 63, the largest of the Smith-Hudsons, has also been piped and has run on both trains for carrying volunteers, stores, etc.

At Portmadoc, the coal stage has been moved to beside the water tank, and a new coal siding has been laid behind. Much re-laying of the dead-end and run-arounds has been completed, whilst at the top the stretch from Whistling Curve down to Llechwedd Coed has now been totally re-laid.

In the Shops, the new floor in the top machine end is being laid in concrete.

As mentioned, *Merddin Emrys* has been in service since July, and has given a good account of herself. She still needs attention to the valves and valve vents, and the centre couplers fitted also require further attention. Running without a cab has proved to be very much more pleasant, even in wet weather, than with the *Earl's* cab (where one side boils and the other gets wet!) On *Merddin Emrys* a coat can be worn to keep dry, without the wearer getting too hot.

28. No. 14's underframe had been unloaded the wrong way round; it was turned fairly easily in the yard. Two of the Smiths wagons (in use for coal), *Merddin Emrys* and *Moelwyn* (now with front pony truck) are also seen in this October view. (A.G.W.Garraway)

1962

NEWS FROM THE LINE - Winter 1962

Boston Lodge has settled down to its winter routine, now that the staff have had their spell of holidays. The floor of the new machine shop has been completed, but there is still some finishing off to do of odd bits and pieces; the machines are being moved into their new locations, and the shaper has been re-assembled. Roofing repairs are being carried out to several of the buildings, whilst fencing work up the line continues. Up in Blaenau, the fence between the tracks at Duffws and Dolgaregddu Street has been almost completely renewed.

The work on No. 14 (L. & B.) proceeds, and the erection of both new and original sections is in progress. The bogies and brake gear are being overhauled, and drawgear—ex-W. & Ll. couplers—fitted. No. 11 has been gutted, and the bare body is completely devoid of floor or underframe. Work is commencing on fabrication of the new steel underframe, onto which the present body will fit. The "seaward" side of No. 22 is being repainted, but nothing much has been done to any of the locomotives.

On the permanent way, Ty Fry curve has been realigned to a more uniform radius; it is one of the few curves on the line where there is sufficient space to allow anything of this nature, and it is surprising that it had been allowed to remain as it was, with two very sharp places. The curve is now of a uniform radius of about 4 chains. Much re-sleepering has been done around Pen Cefn, and rails have been lifted from the old Votty & Bowydd wharf at the back of Minffordd yard for use elsewhere. The turnout in the bushes here was earmarked for Pen Cob Junction, as it was found to be made up of first class bull-head rail; this wharf was only laid out in the early 1920's, yet they indulged in the extravagance of making a new turnout for the job. Some of the siding rail is recalled by Will Jones to have been lifted from the curve by Tan-y-Bwlch bridge when that section was itself renewed in bull-head.

Work continues on the curves and turnouts by Boston Lodge, though some jobs await ballast from B.R. for completion. The increasing use of ballast-cleaning machines by B.R. is making less available for disposal; however, our Western friends are coming to the rescue, so that there should be plenty for future volunteers to unload. It is hoped that a good party will be at work after Christmas, when the remaining rail in the tunnel is to be lifted and placed ready for relaying.

29. Over the New Year, a volunteer party was staying at the Blaenau end, meeting at the Tunnel to help load materials which had been prepared before the holiday. Unfortunately seasonal weather conditions meant that it took longer to get up than was hoped; at some places shovels had to be used to proceed. (A.G.W.Garraway)

30. Some shunting was done with difficulty at Dduallt but one unplanned benefit of the day's toil was this picture that served as the Garraway Christmas card at the end of the year. (A.G.W.Garraway)

31. Having beaten back nature's invasion of FR property, it was important to maintain the advantage gained. This improved weedkilling wagon had a handpump for spraying walls, in addition to the usual spray bar for the track. (A.G.W.Garraway)

32. Nos. 11, 12, 22 and the two ex-WHR coaches had timber underframes all feeling the effects of anno domini, and did not meet the standards required. In the foreground is part of the new underframe for no. 11 and, behind, is the Lynton & Barnstaple coach, no. 14, partly reassembled. (A.G.W.Garraway)

33. The FR, like most of the Heritage Railways, is always on the scrounge for useful materials discarded by others. Similarly, our printers spotted a large screw press in our offices. They could make good use of it and so it had a new life in the binding department. Prior to the advent of stencil duplicators, the FR had used it for a letter copying process. (A.G.W.Garraway)

34. In 1962, the work on the floor of the erecting shop was continued at the northern end, the area now occupied mainly by the welders. This proved a most trying job as the area to be concreted was between those used by the engineering staff, so the two groups of workers were constantly getting in each other's way. Coupled with this was the added complication of a large concrete block which

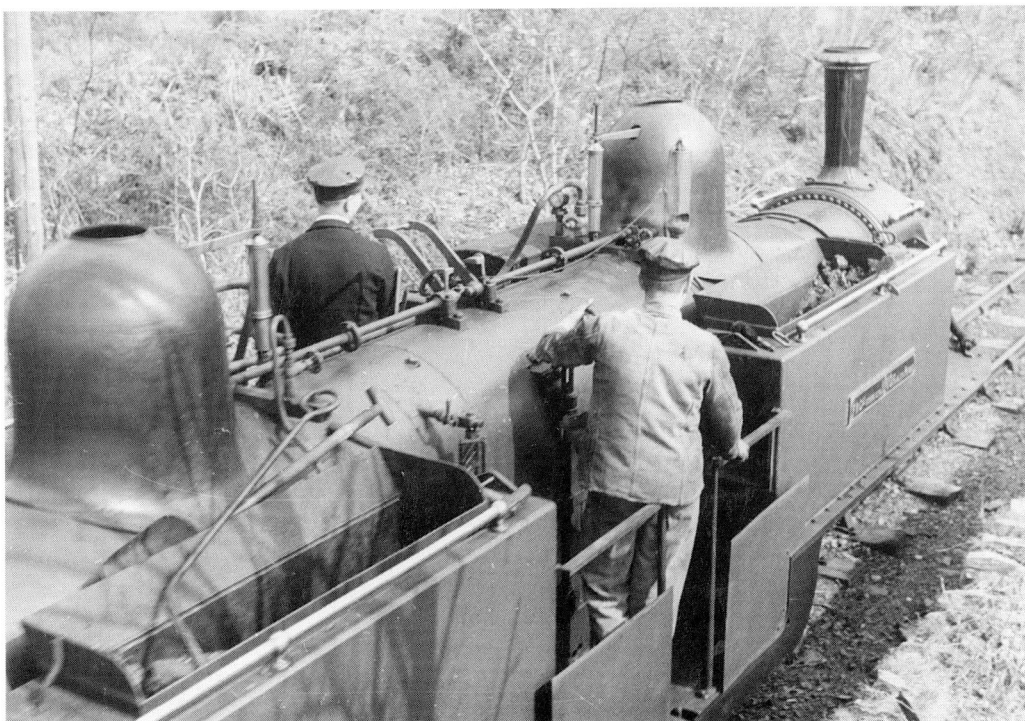

had to be removed before the work could be started. This had to be jacked up and then slid along rails laid up onto a flat truck. The track into this part of the works was incorporated into the floor and extended across the shop. The work was completed in about three weeks. (J.F.Andrews)

35. Another milestone was reached at Easter, when the first nine-coach train was run. *Merddin Emrys* is seen heading it and traversing Cei Mawr. *Moelwyn* and wagon no. 63 are behind the locomotive. (J.F.Andrews)

NEWS FROM THE LINE - Spring 1962

The winter programme has continued apace, although the snow and severe weather that heralded in the New Year affected the F.R. as it affected others. This period saw a large gang from Cambridge University helping to lift the remaining bull-head rail from Moelwyn tunnel; on some days the trains taking them to work had to dig their way through the cuttings, resulting in much waste of time.

This bull-head rail has been placed at various points ready for relaying, and the length from Gysgfa to Cutting Budr has already been re-railed. Pen Cob points have been relaid, with the addition of a short spur replacing the catch points (to allow shunting into Glan-y-mor yard when the junction is locked), and digging out of the Minffordd Cemetery stretch is now almost completed.

At Boston Lodge, *Merddin Emrys* has had the valves in the bottom end bogie refaced. and drains have been fitted also to the valve chests. *Prince's* firebox repairs have now been finally completed, and the cylinders are expected very shortly. *Earl of Merioneth* is being retubed by fitters from the Vulcan Foundry.

Carriage No. 14 (L. & B.) is well on with assembly; most of the side sections, together with the ends, have been erected, and the brake gear re-assembled using a new train pipe. The new underframe for No. 11 (Observation Car) has been completed and placed under the body, which is being repanelled in the normal F.R. manner. No. 17 is receiving attention to its "seaward" side.

36. As already seen on the cover, *Merddin Emrys* ran initially devoid of weather protection after its rebuild. This picture gives a clear view of the two regulators which can be operated with one hand when required. (J.F.Andrews)

37. Problems can be expected when vehicles are put into service partially finished, as was the case on the AGM Special on 28th April. The coaches were inclined to change shape when full! (J.F.Andrews)

38. The pointwork at the entrance to Boston Lodge Works was relaid and a headshunt provided in place of catch points. This meant that it was possible for movement between Glan-y-Mor Yard and the main yard without having to obtain a token and block the main line. The running line points were renewed in May 1963. (A.G.W.Garraway)

39. The underframe seen in picture no. 32 has received the body of no. 11, which now awaits new panels. The vehicle returned to traffic at Easter, although the first class compartment had to be finished during the following week. (A.G.W.Garraway)

40. It had been hoped that 1962 would see an improvement in the motive power situation. The two Fairlies were running and *Prince* was being rebuilt with new cylinders ready for the peak season. However, these hopes were soon dashed when *Merddin Emrys* developed serious problems with firebox crown stays and the *Earl of Merioneth* (renamed from *Taliesin*) was not running as well as would have been liked, due to axlebox problems. The immediate solution was to hire the Penrhyn Quarry Railway's *Linda*. She is seen in Minffordd Yard, on 14 July, being prepared for unloading from a BR wagon. (A.G.W.Garraway)

NEWS FROM THE LINE - Summer 1962

Easter, very late this year, produced some extremely heavy traffic, in spite of poor weather beforehand. During May, the trains have continued to be exceedingly well patronised, and the inclusion in the time-table of the Tuesday trains run in connection with coach tours has proved most profitable.

On the track, Pantuffern has been completely relaid, with bull-head rail from the tunnel, new sleepers and ballast, the track being lifted some inches to clear the usual lumps of rock, the cause of so many F.R. bumps. The mineral line at Minffordd is being relaid; good progress was made over Easter and the work will be completed when the train service precludes work on the main line. The stretch down from Lloc Meirig Crossing past the cemetery is currently being attended to; here again the track is being lifted off the rock to give a smoother ride. The trans-shipping of ballast from B.R. at Minffordd is now simplified by a new ballast grid designed by permanent-way man Paul Dukes.

On the motive power side, the reassembly of *Prince* has begun at last, all the necessary components now being available. Difficulties were encountered in the retubing of *Earl of Merioneth*, due to the firebox tubeplate holes having gone oval, necessitating the fitment of ferrules. Thanks to a good effort by the fitters from Vulcan Foundry, the Fairlie was steaming—and steaming well—for the A.G.M., but the top bogie has since been removed for attention to axle-boxes, four new ones being provided, whilst the frames are being rebolted to the rear ballast box.

Coach No. 11 (the observation) was returned to traffic at Easter on its new steel underframe, and with fresh external lower panels, but the upholstery in the enlarged first-class compartment was not finished off until later in the week, in time for the A.G.M. Hydraulic dampers, together with the bolster springs outside the main bogie frames, have produced a very steady-riding vehicle. The rear end is now painted the same colours as the sides, except for the buffer beam which is signal red. The smart appearance of this coach so disgraced No. 12 (the buffet) that the latter vehicle has also been given a fresh coat of green paint, and, together with coaches 18 and 20, has been fitted with outside springing and dampers.

Steady progress is being maintained on No. 14 (the Lynton and Barnstaple) and the body framework is virtually complete. It is to be square-beaded below the waist, with no intermediate moulding, similar to No. 15, and the curve of the roof has been increased to give more headroom in the centre of the coach. The twenty-four volt electrical equipment will include a refrigerator for ice cream. The usual B.R. dynamo will be fitted, but an emergency charging plug will enable the batteries to be charged at Portmadoc if necessary, an interlock onto the vacuum brake system ensuring that the train cannot be moved while the cable is connected. This coach will be used as buffet car for the main train and will have a guard's compartment at the bottom end. No. 12 will then be available as buffet van for the second train.

The four-wheelers have also received attention in the last few weeks. No. 6 has been fully repainted in green and ivory, whilst Nos. 4 and 5 have had their matchboard panels replaced by ply and are being similarly repainted, to give a smart rake of coaches.

The Crossley engine, which for years has driven the erecting shop shafting and machines, was getting more and more temperamental, and finally refused to do anything at all. A small motor was therefore installed, and as from 6th April, the shafting has been electrically driven. This is one more stage in the general modernisation programme of the workshop.

S. and T. work continues on the Portmadoc–Minffordd remote control wire and on the Penrhyn–Tan-y-Bwlch staff wire; the latter should be in operation for the peak season. Work is also in hand above Tan-y-Bwlch and it is hoped to put up permanent wiring as far as Coed-y-Bleddiau in August.

41. No sooner was *Linda* unloaded and taken to Boston Lodge than she was filled with water and lit up. On 15th July, the yard had three engines in steam, the first time that this had happened for very many years. (A.G.W.Garraway)

42. Boston Lodge buildings were all in a parlous state; like so much else it was a question of patching up as far as possible. It was extremely awkward to get vehicles into the Joiners Shop at the back of the top yard. The building was beyond economic repair and started to fall down. *Moelwyn* and a rope were used to pull it down completely before anyone was hurt. (A.G.W.Garraway)

43. The hearse van had been stored in the better part of the Joiners Shop. When the middle room at Harbour Station was made into a small museum it was found that it would just go through the door. (A.G.W.Garraway)

NEWS FROM THE LINE - Autumn 1962

Traffic results are always uppermost in our minds at this time of year. By the end of June the fortnight-late start to the season had been made good, and the end of July saw a spectacular increase in traffic over last year which was not far short of the record-breaking 1960 (T.V. year) figures. The August peak was slightly down on last year, but by the middle of September more passengers had already been booked on the railway than during the whole of 1961.

The new timetable has proved a great improvement; the trains have been much more uniformly loaded and only on the odd occasion has there been any difficulty in accommodating all the intending passengers. Nevertheless, it is impossible to carry much more traffic in August, except at week-ends, unless we get more stock—and more first class. During June the trains were very crowded and a heavier service could be introduced to advantage, providing sufficient staff were available.

The heartening traffic figures, coupled with our prophecy in the last *Magazine* that the Railway would "shortly have three locomotives in service together for the first time for more than twenty years" may have tended to give the impression that the season has gone smoothly and without any operating difficulties. Let us hastily dispel any such notions. It has, without doubt, been the most hectic operating season since the Simplex struggled across the Cob with two coaches back in 1955.

The main, though by no means only, headache has been the locomotive situation. Immediately *Earl of Merioneth* had returned to traffic on June 23rd, *Merddin Emrys* was brought in for attention to a loose eccentric sheave. When that had been dealt with, *Earl* was brought in for a similar defect, and while it was being repaired—a lengthy job involving the removal of the wheels—*Merddin*'s firebox began to give cause for concern, leaking badly from the crown stays. On Wednesday, July 4th, it was an effort to keep any water in the

boiler at all, and with the peak service due to start in four days time, *Merddin* had to be withdrawn from active service—a bitter and unexpected blow. Due to the method of construction, repair was obviously not going to be easy, and with our Vulcan friends away on holiday, there was no hope of getting the Fairlie back into service for the busy season. *Earl of Merioneth*, intended mainly for spare engine duties this summer, therefore became Top Link engine, literally overnight, as an all-night session was needed to get her back into traffic on the Thursday morning.

Efforts to get *Prince* running again were then redoubled, but it was obvious that *Earl* and *Prince* could not be expected to cope with the heavy summer timetable without assistance. Discussions having previously taken place with the Penrhyn Quarry people regarding the purchase of their main line engines when the line was closed, they were approached again, and *Linda* was hired for the duration of the Summer, being loaded onto B.R. at Port Penrhyn on Friday, July 13th, unloaded by the P.W. staff at Minffordd on the Saturday evening and reaching Boston Lodge on the Sunday morning. That same evening she was steamed and attached to the six-coach main train in order to test her capabilities. Unfortunately, having reached Cei Mawr, she was obliged to return, as remaining water and coal supplies appeared to be insufficient to complete the journey to Tan-y-Bwlch with an assured safety margin. Nevertheless, it was at once apparent that this locomotive fulfilled high expectations in terms of tractive effort.

Meanwhile, with only one serviceable steam locomotive, there had been no alternative but to defer the introduction of the peak Summer timetable, and, instead, last year's four trains (10-30, 12-30 2-30 and 4-30) had been run, hauled by *Earl of Merioneth*, together with a *Moelwyn*-hauled "Flea" at 3-00 p.m. No complaints were heard from passengers concerning this treatment.

Prince was steamed on July 11th, but on his first trial he came to Portmadoc without the regulator being opened; the cause was found to be due to the failure of the joint between the regulator head and the steam pipe inside the boiler. This involved stripping all the dome, with the attendant anxiety of dropping a vital piece inside, and re-machining the joint face. None of the lathes would swing the regulator casting, and finally a Heath Robinson method was adopted, involving the rotation of the casting by hand on the slotter table, with the Myford lathe top slide mounted on the ram, itself locked solid.

On Sunday, July 15th, *Earl*, *Linda* and *Prince* were all in steam, the latter working the advertised train, and the full Summer service was commenced next day. *Prince*, however, was far from perfect, and it was some time before all the bugs were finally sorted out; the ejector, transferred back from *Merddin Emrys*, refused to function properly, and one injector body was found to be cracked and had to be repaired. The sound of the blast has been changed considerably by the rebuilding, as a little lead has been given to the valves. The engine's appearance, too, has been altered, the outer framing being altered so as to take the drawbar pull through it, instead of this being transmitted through the firebox. Instead of stepping up in the centre to support the saddle tank, the outer frame remains level from smokebox to footplate, leaving a space underneath the saddle tank.

With two steam engines in reasonable condition, and both steam and diesel power in reserve, the full service would have appeared to have run smoothly, at least to the casual observer, but nevertheless there have been some very anxious moments in the operating department. Noteworthy is the incident which befell the 10-30 a.m. up train on Wednesday, July 25th, for just after passing Pen-y-Bryn Halt a large rock dislodged itself from a garden wall and fell against the side of the Buffet Car, damaging the footboards, whence it rolled along the side of the vehicle, finally to force itself under the Observation Car, derailing the rear bogie and smashing three axle boxes. The Observation Car passengers were reseated in the rest of the train, which then continued, minus the rear vehicle. The 11-45 a.m. was allowed to proceed from Portmadoc as far as Pen-y-Bryn, and here passengers were 'exchanged' with those from the main train, who had been discharged at Penrhyn, just above the blockage. Most of the passengers seemed to enjoy the novelty of walking along the track, and the operation was successfully completed without incident. After some energetic work by the P.W. gang, through running was restored just after noon, and by 3·00 p.m. the trains were back on normal schedule, but it was not until the small hours of the morning that repairs were completed to the Observation Car.

Some two weeks later, on Thursday, August 9th, to be exact, the 10·30 a.m. departure was delayed by an event of an entirely different nature. About 8·30 a.m. a lorry driver, with a part load of cement to deliver to Boston Lodge Works, was directed thence along the *top* of the Cob! According to him, all went well until nearly half-way across, when our track slowly slewed him against the wall on the footpath side. He was then unable to go forward or back, and *Moelwyn* found him in this state. A hasty return to Boston Lodge for packing enabled the lorry to get its off-side wheels inside the track, but then its spring shackle got jammed in the rails. However, with stones as packing, progress was made slowly, and so it came to pass that, some time later, passengers for the morning train witnessed a strange procession heading over the Cob towards the station. First came one six-wheeled lorry in reverse, *Moelwyn* followed, and back-marker was *Earl of Merioneth* ready to make a belated start with the train.

Then on Friday, August 17th, came the incident which was to cause concern for the welfare of the remainder of the Summer service. *Prince*, with the 11-45 a.m. train, ground to a halt at Hafod-y-Llyn with faulty valve setting and could not be restarted. Diesel power took over the 'third class only' train and *Prince*'s valves were reset over the week-end, but no cause could be found for the trouble. Some trepidation was felt on Monday morning, and *Linda* was steamed as a stand-by; this precaution was soon proved justified.

Very briefly, a broken piston head was found to be the cause of the trouble, and only a 'bodge' repair could be effected. A new piston and rod are being manufactured, but until the engine can be taken out of service for a few days machining cannot very easily be completed. Meanwhile *Prince* was back at work next day, but at reduced

44. The wheel-drop that was completed in the Long Shed in November 1959 was to prove its worth with *Linda*. The former is on the equipment in July following problems with the solid bronze axleboxes, which were not intended for high speed passenger running. (J.L.Alexander)

1963

45. In Blaenau Ffestiniog further alterations to the road layout started in January. The first to affect the FR had been in 1955 when its line between the London Midland Region station (centre) and the Western Region station was severed to permit the construction of an access road to Tanygrisiau Power Station. Now a bridge had to be constructed to carry the road over a new line to be built to connect the two BR termini and also over the FR link between the LMR goods yard and the Maenofferen Quarry. This line carried slate traffic until 3rd November 1962. (A.G.W.Garraway)

efficiency, finding a full load just a bit too much to handle. To help timekeeping, therefore, particularly with the bus connections at Tan-y-Bwlch in mind, *Linda* has been steamed almost daily, double-heading with *Prince* frequently on the 2-15 p.m. and on two occasions handling a train on her own. She has the edge on *Prince* for haulage capacity, though with her present regulator it is difficult to control her considerable power, and there is a lack of water capacity should any delay or slipping take place. It is hoped that negotiations for her to remain will be successful, and if so, minor alterations will soon get over these difficulties. 60-100 lbs. per square inch pressure is adequate for anything she has so far been used on her. The valve setting, by Festiniog standards, is hopeless, as she runs in full gear; resetting will not be easy, but this will be put right if she remains.

Before leaving the operational side, mention must be made of the R.C.T.S. special Festiniog Rail Tour on Sunday, July 22nd. A feature of this tour was that approximately 180 passengers were to travel in each direction on the 'third class only' train, the original contingent having split at Llandudno Junction. *Prince* arrived at Tan-y-Bwlch with the empty stock, ready for the scheduled 2-15 p.m. departure, but due to serious delays, culminating in the diesel railcar breaking an axle and becoming derailed at Pont-y-Pant, the party did not arrive at Tan-y-Bwlch until 3-35 p.m. By this time, the ordinary service train was also ready to leave, and to avoid further delay it was decided to combine the trains. The R.C.T.S. party therefore had the unique experience of travelling in a train consisting of the entire passenger-carrying stock of the Festiniog Railway together with both its operational engines. For the record, *Earl of Merioneth* led the procession, proudly displaying the R.C.T.S. headboard. Then came the six bogie coaches of the service train, followed by *Prince*, the two four-wheeled brake vans, the quarrymen's coach, four four-wheelers, No. 22 and the two Welsh Highland coaches, *Prince* being in the middle to overcome coupling difficulties with No. 2 van. Quite a sight on any day of the week!

The Lynton and Barnstaple coach (No. 14) has been completed structurally, and on Friday evening, August 17th, *Earl of Merioneth* ran a train consisting of No. 20, the L. & B. and No. 11 (the formation which will normally be used) through Garnedd Tunnel. There were sighs of relief from the design staff when it passed through without incident, confirming their calculations and earlier tests. The return journey in the dark demonstrated the superiority of its lighting; No. 20 was given 24 volt bulbs for the occasion and the L. & B. itself was brilliant. The mounting of the dynamo had been something of a problem, due to the restricted clearances underneath, but this also proved satisfactory on test, while the riding of the vehicle was quite superb and there was no spillage from any of the test glasses or cups carried.

Bogie Coach No. 21, built by Ashbury in 1896, the remains of which have been standing in a very dilapidated condition in Glan-y-Mor Yard for some time, has now been dismantled. It was quite unsuitable for rebuilding, but certain parts have been carefully stored away for future use when other coaches require rebuilding. The bogies from this coach are being used, under the Welsh Highland No. 26.

On the Permanent Way there has been little relaying, though quite a few sleepers have been put in here and there as weak places have developed. Above Tan-y-Bwlch, a little more digging out has been done, and the very wet cutting above Coed-y-Bleiddiau has been dug out and ditched by the Enfield boys, thereby earning the name of "Tadpole Cutting".

At Boston Lodge there have been great and startling changes. The Joiners' Shop started to fall down and had become highly dangerous, so it was systematically demolished. During the process, however, the corrugated portion of the Blacksmith's Shop fell down in sympathy! The repairs to the back wall of the Brass Foundry have been expedited so that much of the spare bits and pieces can be stored therein. The Saw Mill has been cleaned out, and a passage to the top yard made where the old Boiler House once was.

Across the line, the Carriage Shed—erstwhile Engine Shed—has been cleaned out, the back pit filled in, and ordinary track is being relaid on top, ready for slewing when this portion of the shed is eventually rebuilt.

In the Erecting Shop, the concreting of the floor has continued from the Machine Shop end through to the first pit, and track has been laid in the concrete so that wagons of materials can be run across the shop. The hacksaw has been motorised and moved, and the drilling machine removed, whilst the large one that was once by the wheel lathe has been rehabilitated and is installed near the main motor, where the Myford lathe was, which, in turn, has been moved behind the planer. The shaper has been installed and motorised at the top end of the shop, opposite the wheel lathe, so that a fairly comprehensive collection of machines is now available and working, ready for tackling the heavy repair jobs ahead.

During the alterations it has been necessary to ask visitors to keep out of the Erecting Shop, but when the work is complete a great change will be seen. As it was, much time was wasted on one occasion due to some thoughtless person walking over the work prepared for concreting and thereby upsetting the levels.

—

46. The LMR terminal building (left) was still fairly new, having been completed in 1956. It was to be the only station in the town for over 20 years after the ex-GWR terminus closed to passengers on 4th January 1960. Freight traffic continued at this station until 27th January 1961 but it was not until 20th April 1964 that the two BR lines were finally connected. The photographer is standing on the site of the FR main line. In 1980 new bridges were required yet again. (A.G.W.Garraway)

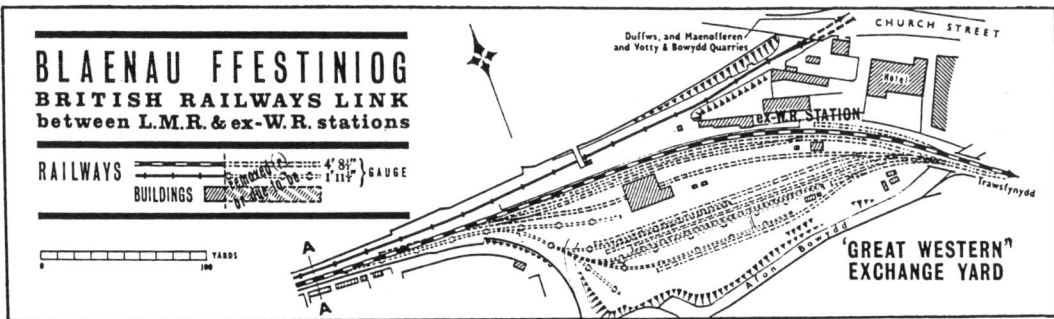

BLAENAU FFESTINIOG
BRITISH RAILWAYS LINK
between L.M.R. & ex-W.R. stations

RAILWAYS

BUILDINGS

'GREAT WESTERN'
EXCHANGE YARD

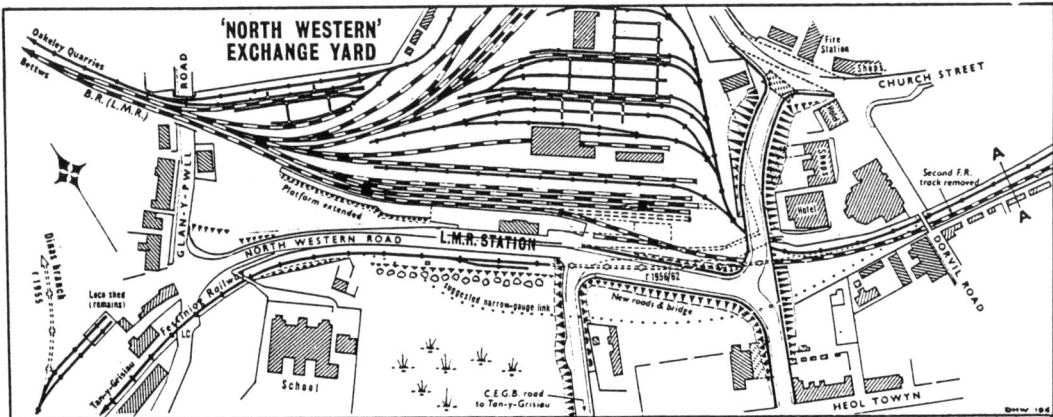

'NORTH WESTERN'
EXCHANGE YARD

47. The L&B coach was dismantled in Devon in May 1959 before movement to Wales. By February, the body had been reassembled to a new profile, with a higher curve to the roof and a new style of panelling. It became no. 14. In the foreground is the new frame for no. 12. (A.G.W.Garraway)

48. No. 12 had become a buffet car in 1957, the first on the FR. At the same time it was fitted with a gangway to no. 11, another "first". It is seen on blocks awaiting the new frame shown in the previous picture. (A.G.W.Garraway)

49. The new frame was constructed five feet longer, so as to give no. 12 an additional compartment and a total length of 30ft. It was photographed on 9th February. The counter was turned from a longitudinal to a transverse position. (A.G.W.Garraway)

NEWS FROM THE LINE - Winter 1963

The final passenger-journey figures came fully up to the expectations expressed in the Autumn issue, reaching 114,047. Of the increase of just on 5,000 over the 1961 figure, 4,350 can be attributed to increased bookings on the Railway itself. B.R. (L.M.R.) with the two circular tours from the north coast gave an extra 400 and the Western Region tours have slightly improved, although still not back to the level of 1960. Although we lost the regular East Kent coach tour due to re-routing, we gained Western Welsh for the Wednesday 4-30— a particularly welcome addition—and Royal Red from Llandudno, and although most of the day trip operators were individually slightly down, in total they were slightly up.

The August peak was far less sharp; in the four weeks up to the 25th, 35,612 journeys were booked on the line compared with 36,049 in 1961, yet the week ending 1st September gave 9,188 compared with 7,043 in 1961, higher than either of the first two weeks in August. As a further indication of the general staggering of holidays, the last two weeks of July gave an increase of 1,600. During August the trains are nearly all full (except at weekends) and until we have more coaches the best way we can increase our traffic is by encouraging the national movement to spread the holiday season; to benefit from this the 1963 timetable is to include a 12·00 from Portmadoc and 1·00 from Tan-y-Bwlch during the whole main season. The 2-30 is being re-timed to 2-20 so that there will be a little more time at Tan-y-Bwlch and also to give an easier path for the running of a relief at 2-55 if needed.

With the end of the season, the permanent way boys have been able to have complete possession of the track again, and to get on with the all-important relaying which has got to be done this winter. Whilst a large number of new sleepers has been put in during the summer, this has, of necessity, been in the nature of first-aid repairs. The first main job has been the complete relaying in Minffordd platform including all the pointwork of the crossover and the curve above the station, and now the curves above Penrhyn level-crossing have also been done. This included the removal of the large tree by Corn Pigyn house, which was endangering the wall.

To speed the p.w. work, an additional pair of hands has been recruited to the gang; Hugh Hodgson, ex-cavalier and mounted policeman, he at present mounts a Land-Rover, but has diverse experience in many aspects of country craft to give that versatility so valuable in an organization such as ours.

After Christmas the stretches from Gysgfa to Sheepfold and Milestone Curve to Tyler's will be completely relaid; we shall want plenty of help to get these dug out and weeded if the programme is to be completed by Easter. This will make the stretch from Cei Mawr to Whistling Curve 100% resleepered apart from two short stretches which have been heavily patched, and it is hoped to bring these up to the 100%-new-sleeper standard by Whitsun.

At Boston Lodge most of the time has been spent in going through the mechanical side of the coaches, overhauling brake gear, fitting new blocks, etc. Most of the bogies have been taken out and the secondary springing fully modified. On the F.R. the weight of the coach has always been carried by a ball centre pivot in a socket on the bogie, side springs being provided inside the bogie frame to keep the body upright. The springing of the coach, therefore, relied entirely upon the primary springs, consisting of a nest of three short coil springs on each axlebox—all right on good track but not very absorbent of shocks. The modification consists in mounting the secondary springs outside the bogie frames, thereby giving a very much wider spacing to assist stability, with shock absorbers to reduce still further any tendency to roll, and in boring out the bogie centre to put the weight entirely on the secondary springs. Whilst some of the coaches had previously been fitted with the modified springing and shock absorbers, completion of the programme will not only give the passengers a very much more comfortable ride but will reduce the shocks and shaking of the coaches themselves, will tend to reduce the wear on the track and, furthermore, will enable these springs to be inspected without jacking the coaches up off their bogies.

The present buffet car (No. 12) has been completely stripped internally and a new steel underframe is being made. At the same time the coach is being lengthened by five feet to give an additional section and a few extra seats.

On the engines, a few jobs have been done on *Prince*, including the provision of two new pistons; experiments to make him steam more reliably have also been made, and tests made with the indicator machine to investigate the steam performance of the cylinders. Unfortunately a broken spring stopped tests before any final conclusion could be arrived at. *Merddin Emrys* has been fitted with weatherboards (namely, the usable portion of her old cab, whose offer as an unusual garden shed to the enthusiast public proved less enticing than hoped) and flared extensions to the top of the bunkers.

Linda was involved in a derailment at Squirrel Crossing on 5th September and incurred slight damage to the eccentrics. She remains in store awaiting the outcome of negotiations with the Penrhyn Quarry people regarding her purchase.

For the coming year the museum display is being completely rearranged, and the hearse van has been inserted, together with the surviving wooden slate wagon, so that these two interesting relics may be more readily seen. Their restoration, and the redecoration of the museum and the adjoining room which has been added to it to extend the display, are being done by some of the lady volunteers, and others as an indoor task for evenings and wet days.

The wealth of news from other departments has tended to obscure the work of the S. & T. Engineer and his parties who, throughout the Summer, pressed on with the electric tablet wire from Minffordd to Tan-y-Bwlch, wiring between weekend services or in the evenings from their "train"—bogie wagon 63, a virtually ideal vehicle for the job. Connection through was made in August, and Minffordd and Tan-y-Bwlch stations rang with unfamiliar bells as the intricacies of the historic Tyer's tablet instruments, obtained from the Admiralty's Lodge Hill & Upnor Railway, were gingerly charted. Work also continued on the telephone system, and permanent wiring now extends to the end of the plantation above Tafarntrip, 500 yards towards Dduallt.

50. The Wickham trolley was reconstructed during the winter and was pictured in February. The device on top is a hand-wound klaxon for audible warning of approach. It ran 10,187 miles to the end of 1969. In the background is the sawmill, just prior to its demolition. (A.G.W.Garraway)

51. *Earl of Merioneth* was in an advanced stage of stripping in March, ready for a major overhaul which was to last until 1967. It included boiler and firebox repairs, together with the manufacture of many new components. (A.G.W.Garraway)

52. *Welsh Pony* required very heavy repairs. She was despatched to an exhibition in Birmingham in March. It was to be 1984 before she was put on a plinth near the entrance to Harbour station. (A.G.W.Garraway)

53. A major landmark in the history of the FR was the "Centenary of Steam" celebrations in May. *Prince* was the star of the show, being one of the original locomotives. This was Press Day on the 22nd. (R.Fisher)

54. To reduce the time taken to relay pointwork, particularly that which is required every day, turnouts were prefabricated in the P.W. yard at Minffordd and brought down on wagons ready to be laid in quickly. This is the turnout to the pit in Boston Lodge bottom yard. (A.G.W.Garraway)

55.   Seldom appearing in FR photographs is the hand-cranked crane in Minffordd Yard. It was rated at 2½ tons capacity, had a wooden jib and was intended for exchange traffic. Staffing of the BR station ceased on 19th October 1964 but the sidings were in use for public traffic until 7th February 1966 and FR consignments until 1972. The FR purchased an ex-GWR 3-ton travelling crane in 1965. (J.L.Alexander)

56.   *Linda* was over the wheel-drop again in June with bearing problems. Behind the jacks, blocks stand on a trolley which is on rails in the pit floor. This enabled the wheelset to be removed sideways. (J.L.Alexander)

57.   On 1st June a new halt was opened just above Tylers Curve by Mr Bibby, then owner of Plas Tan-y-bwlch. It has since become an education centre and the gardens are open to the public in season so the halt does get a little more use. The general manager stands between Mr and Mrs Bibby. (A.G.W.Garraway)

58.   Traffic was so heavy on 5th June that a 10-coach train was worked, hauled by *Merddin Emrys* and *Prince*. The dry-stone embankment of Cei Mawr presented the ideal location to record it from the footplate. Afforestation ruined this viewpoint subsequently. (A.G.W.Garraway)

59.   In the roof of the Pattern Shop were the sections of track of the miniature railway which C.E.Spooner used to operate in the grounds of his house. One day a young Oxford graduate, Nick Knight, arrived and said that he had something in the boot of his Mini which might be of interest. Resting on rugs was *Topsy*, which Spooner had run on the track. It is now proudly displayed in the FR museum on one of the sections of track; it had been built in 1869 by W.Williams, the locomotive foreman at Boston Lodge and is being unveiled by Bill Broadbent (left) and Alan Pegler. (N.F.Gurley coll.)

60. More wagons arrived in June, this time from RAF Alrewas in Staffordshire. They were steel-bodied four-wheelers, in good condition and ideal for ballast. They had been built by Robert Hudson Ltd in 1952. (A.G.W.Garraway)

61. By the middle of July, *Linda* was fully equipped with vacuum ejector and a flood injector. For the first time there were three engines available for traffic; *Linda* is seen working the 3.00pm non-stop to Tan-y-bwlch, named "Y Cymro". Open wagon no. 63 was included for the benefit of the S&T Department. (A.G.W.Garraway)

62. Allan Garraway eases *Linda* into the loop at Penrhyn to pass a delayed down train. A steam locomotive failure meant the down train had to be rescued by the two diesels. (N.F.Gurley)

NEWS FROM THE LINE - Summer 1963

The Centenary issue of the Magazine only carried news of a general nature, and we therefore have a six months' period to cover in detail. During that time there has been quite a change on the locomotive front. The 1962 season ended with *Earl of Merioneth* needing an extensive overhaul to reach the exacting standards we now set ourselves and *Prince* in potentially good shape but needing attention to several parts. *Merddin Emrys* was awaiting fire-box repairs and *Linda*, if indeed she was to remain on the Festiniog locomotive strength, needed repair and modification.

Since then good progress has been made, particularly during the early months of this year when the freezing weather tended to divert labour from outside pursuits. At the time of going to press towards the end of June, the position is as follows:

Merddin Emrys: The fire-box repairs were carried out during the winter, enabling the engine to return to traffic for Easter. The spectacle plates have been taken from the old cab, but no roof is provided, though bars have been fitted between the weatherboards so that storm sheets can be arranged. A Dreadnought vacuum ejector has been fitted, replacing the old "B" type which was obsolete and beyond repair. The engine is now in full livery and is ready to take the lion's share of the season's traffic. As a machine, she is not a match for *Earl*; the cylinders are in a poor state and although both bottom end ones were removed during the spring and rejointed, there is still far too much obvious blow-through straight from live steam to exhaust, which all represents waste of steam and water. Unfortunately, also, when the engine was rebuilt the opportunity was not taken to enlarge the tanks, with the result that water capacity is extremely tight for heavy trains. With No. 14 in the formation, seven bogies is *Merddin's* unassisted limit at present.

Prince: The veteran has started his second century in fine style. The Kylchap cowl has so improved the draughting efficiency that the blast pipe orifice has been enlarged from $2\frac{1}{4}$ in. to $2\frac{3}{8}$ in. with consequent reduction in back pressure. Mesh screens have been fitted to reduce the spark-throwing to which he was prone. With a "brick arch" of Stein's special cement in the fire-box, any fireman can contrive to make him blow off going up through the woods, and slack or a bit of clinker present no worries. The tubes are the originals of 1944, and are slowly giving out; several have been changed at the bottom, but such is the steaming efficiency that he can get by with one or two leaking until attention can be given. *Prince* also has had a repaint.

Earl of Merioneth: Boiler and fire-box repairs are still in hand, priority having been given to the other locomotives to ensure that they were available at the start of the season. Most of the mechanical work has been done.

Linda: Although she is still officially on loan, several modifications have been carried out. The wheels have been re-tyred to Festiniog standards, a Dreadnought vacuum ejector fitted and the regulator modified. At present she is running with coal wagon 38, which was one of the England wooden-framed tenders, but the remaining steel England tender is being overhauled and modified like *Prince's* (but with a water tank) for permanent attachment.

Internal Combustion Engines: Simplex now starts by electrical means. After the frantic cranking of early days this seems something of a luxury, but it is essential now a diesel engine has been fitted. *Moelwyn* continues to give faithful service.

Unfortunately, John (Borth) Roberts has been off sick from some weeks which has depleted the works labour strength; we all wish him a speedy recovery.

More remarkable have been the improvements to the carriage stock during the winter. Not only has the "new" buffet car entered revenue-earning service, but the fourth and last "bow-sider", No. 19, has been rebuilt, partly under contract, and should be ready for service during July. Additionally, the old buffet car, No. 12, has been rebuilt (for the nth time even under the present administration!). Fitted on a steel underframe of "standard" 30 ft. length, it has acquired thereby an additional compartment. The seating has been altered to give fourteen seats, in pairs, on the seaward side of the aisle and seven single seats on the other side, with tables to some units—a similar layout to No. 14. The floor has been lowered, except over the bogies, and the counter has been arranged transversely. It has been fitted for the service of draught "Tankard" and carries other bottled beers, but otherwise the refreshment facilities are as before.

All first class compartments have been fitted with very smart specially woven carpets, bearing the Railway's crest. Third class comfort is also being improved with the fitting of simple but quite effective upholstery.

Progress has been made on the 'rebuilding of No. 16, which, apart from the small and broken-framed No. 10, is the last of the Festiniog bogie coaches to be tackled.

It would not be out of place, whilst on the subject of coaching stock, to give some publicity to a small handful of oily cotton waste, which has now been placed in a polythene bag and pinned to a notice board in Boston Lodge. Though apparently quite innocuous, it got into the wrong place and was therefore the cause of much "humbug". When all the carriage wheels were sorted out during the autumn, the poorest were put under No. 26, which consequently has only been used when absolutely necessary; viz. on A.G.M. day, on Whit Tuesday and on a recent occasion when the 12-00 noon train was heavily loaded. In each case, brake trouble was experienced, but it was not until the last occasion that it became obvious that 26 had a partial blockage in the train pipe. After the pipe had been partly stripped, the offending lump of waste was blown out of an inaccessible portion with the aid of compressed air (it emerged with considerable force). The moral for all engaged in shunting operations is obvious: *keep everything clear of vacuum pipes*. A little carelessness on somebody's part had been the cause of three unfortunate delays and it could easily have been more. No. 26 has now been fitted with brand new wheels and will, no doubt, see plenty of service in the peak season.

The wagon stock has been augmented in recent weeks. Two granite and two slab wagons have been brought down from the Maenofferen Quarry at Blaenau and four more granites are expected soon, whilst from Alrewas, Staffordshire, have come a couple of Hudson bogies and sixteen four-wheeled steel-sided wagons. These latter are sorely needed for helping to carry ballast; in the winter ballast always seems to arrive when the p.w. work doesn't require it, but never when it does! There is no labour to spare for double-handling—or convenient space for stacking—so contrary to B.R. modernisation ideas, more wagons are essential to use as mobile stores. The first of the Alrewas bogies has had its bogies replaced by the German roller-bearing bogies ex Brookes Quarry. After the body had been overhauled and painted by the Hants and Sussex Group Whit week working party, it entered service on 14th June, numbered 68, being loaded with coal by the London Area Group party next day.

Hard work has been done on many sections of the track throughout the winter and spring. The most easily noticeable improvements will be at the entrance to Boston Lodge, where the pointwork has been extensively relaid. To avoid disruption of traffic, one set of points was prefabricated. Many tons of ballast have been put down, particularly between Cei Mawr and Tylers, whilst many other routine, rarely reported jobs such as fencing, ditching, weed-killing, keying-up and general tidying-up have all taken many man-hours' work. The permanent way gang has lost Hugh Hodgson and gained Michael Hartley and Norman Gurley.

The Signals and Telegraph Department have been devoting most of their working hours to the Cob. The Gwynedd River Board are strengthening the seaward side, and to give their crane and other equipment plenty of room our telegraph poles and overhead wires

are being taken out. Instead, one multi-core cable is being laid against the outside base of the concrete wall. This should give better service with less maintenance than the overhead wires.

Though the operating season has not yet reached its peak, it has already had some exciting moments. The first was on A.G.M. day, when all available stock had to be pressed into service. *Merddin Emrys* got to Tan-y-Bwlch without too much effort with seven bogies, but *Prince* couldn't cope with a train which included the half-finished 19 with binding brakes and 26 with partially blocked vacuum pipe. The train was left "in the woods" while *Prince* ran to Tan-y-Bwlch for water, and *Merddin* went down for the train. The Fairlie was fully extended bringing it up, but apart from the inevitable late running the rest of the day's programme passed without incident.

The effects of the extra publicity were felt at Whitsun; the weather was perfect and Portmadoc was full of holiday-makers. On the Tuesday the 2-20 train had to be loaded to ten well-filled bogie coaches, motive power being provided by *Prince* and *Merddin Emrys*. Nine coaches were needed on the same train next day, No. 26 being left off with a consequent improvement in time-keeping, but seven sufficed on Thursday. It is too early in the season to compare the passenger figures with last year's, but there would seem to be a clear increase so far.

The weekday service until 6th July consists of four trains. *Merddin Emrys* has been handling the 10-45 and 2-20 departures, and *Prince* the 12-00 and 4-30. When double-heading was necessary on the 2-20, *Prince* was able to run down light from Tan-y-Bwlch to ensure prompt departure of the 4-30—Mr. Spooner's continuous gradient still has its advantages.

Difficulties arose from an unexpected quarter one day soon after Whitsun, when it was found that the water supply had been cut off from Boston Lodge. Fortunately there was sufficient water in *Merddin Emrys*'s tanks for the Fairlie to be steamed and the 10-45 left on time, but *Prince* could not be lit up until he had been towed to Portmadoc for water then back to Boston Lodge, and as a result, the 12-00 train left thirty minutes late. Passengers were kept abreast of the difficulties by means of the excellent public address system at Harbour Station and seemed amused by the explanations, as they did on another occasion when the guard was late on duty for the 10-45.

63. To enable *Linda* to carry a little reserve of water, one of the old England tenders, in use as coal wagon no. 38, had a couple of oil drums fitted for water and a compartment made for coal. The small bunker on the engine had been removed to give space for the reverser and the vacuum ejector. (A.G.W.Garraway)

With the end of the peak season almost here (at time of writing) it is possible, without tempting providence too much, to look back on the smoothest, as well as most prosperous, season on the Railway, for many years. From the motive power angle, this has been largely due to the availability of a spare steam locomotive for service throughout the season, for the first time under the present administration. *Linda* has unquestionably justified herself this year by providing not only the much-needed reserve of motive power but also by giving valuable flexibility in the locomotive department.

After the phenomenal number of bookings in Whit-week, a long period of dull weather caused a slight decline in traffic which lasted well into July, but totals nevertheless held up on last year. Then came August Bank Holiday weekend, and the start of a remarkable month. There were over 400 bookings on the Sunday (including, of course, a good number of members) and Bank Holiday Monday (previously relatively quiet) produced 1,173 bookings. The Tuesday figure of 1,411 broke records, but Wednesday was wet and only 573 tickets were sold. The week was eight short of the record number of bookings, established in 1960, but set up a new record of 10,422 passenger-journeys.

The next week produced nothing really exciting, but, as nearly always, the third week in August proved to be the season's busiest. All five week-days gave bookings of over 1,100, and the total of 6,756 bookings, 12,571 journeys, completely smashed all previous records. It was fortunate indeed that the load was spread evenly throughout the week and that two more coaches had been brought into service since 1962. Another good week followed, and by 4th September last year's total figure had been passed. All these figures exclude British Railways and coach excursion bookings, which are also up on last year.

There have been some changes in the working of the trains as the traffic has developed. At first, the main train, with Buffet Car No. 14 and Observation Car No. 11, worked the 10-30, 1-05 and 3-00 (non-stop *Y Cymro*) as advertised, with *Merddin Emrys* for motive power, but it soon became obvious that the crowds were mostly on the other three trains, which, with *Prince*, were heavily loaded. The workings were therefore reversed, and in early August *Prince* was handling the three trains mentioned, with coaches 12 (buffet), 20, 19, 22 and one W.H.R., while *Merddin* took 11, 14, 18, 17, 15, a W.H.R. and, when necessary, the six four-wheelers, on the 11-45, 2-15 and 4-30 departures.

During the record-breaking week another adjustment was needed, as five bogies were proving insufficient on *Y Cymro*. To give a few extra seats therefore the four-wheelers were exchanged for a W.H.R. The resulting formation of four bogies and six four-wheelers was a bit of a struggle for *Prince*, particularly on the thirty-five-minute non-stop, and so *Linda* was put into regular week-day service. This busy week also coincided with the first week of the "Tadpoles" visit and as some of them returned to Portmadoc with their equipment on the 4-07 down train, No. 63 (the piped open Hudson) was included in *Y Cymro* formation—a rare example of a "mixed" named train.

The introduction of *Y Cymro* produced some useful publicity, the engine carrying an aluminium headboard with white letters on green and red background and surround. The first run was done by *Prince* in thirty-three minutes, with the (then) premier train of 11, 14, 20, 18 and 17.

As mentioned briefly in the last Magazine, there was a shock just before the start of the peak season, when *Merddin Emrys* split the points at the headshunt coming out of Boston Lodge on Thursday, 4th July. This caused a heavy delay to the 10-45 train, though most of the passengers waited, with coffee etc., served from the buffet car. The tragedy was that the derailment had broken off the bottom steam pipe elbow, a portion of the steam chest casting. *Prince* and *Moelwyn* worked a combined 10-45/12-00 and *Prince* assisted *Merddin* (with top end only working) on the 2-20. Next day *Prince* took the main trains and *Merddin* coped with the light 12-00, and over the week-end a newly-fabricated elbow was studded and bolted onto the casting. The peak season started on the Monday, with some trepidation as to how *Merddin* would function, but the repair proved satisfactory for the best part of the season. Nevertheless, the Fairlie had her troubles, particularly from a leaking foundation ring, and a broken steam pipe which had to be very hurriedly repaired, and there was much relief on 14th July when *Linda* was satisfactorily worked on a test passenger train. Thereafter she saw a good deal of service at week-ends, enabling more leisurely maintenance and repairs to be carried out on the regular pair.

During Bank Holiday week, timekeeping suffered, particularly with *Merddin*, due to the use of a poor batch of coal. The position became so acute that a wagon of best Yorkshire coal was borrowed from British Railways. This gave excellent steaming performance on all engines—but a complete smoke screen everywhere. A consignment of our usual coal, from Park Colliery, Treorchy, arrived soon afterwards, and the air cleared.

On Friday, 9th August, the royal train conveying H.M. the Queen and Prince Philip from Pwllheli to Harlech was due to pass through Minffordd about 5-45 p.m., and *Prince* was duly stationed on the mineral siding within sight of the royal party. Passengers on the 5-30 down alighted at Minffordd to see the royal special go through, and *Merddin Emrys*'s train returned later to pick them up. The royal train, hauled by two gleaming *Manors*, passed through some fifty minutes late. The following day, the Queen opened the C.E.G.B. pumped storage hydro-electric scheme and power station at Tan-y-Grisiau, Mr. and Mrs. A. F. Pegler being among the guests.

Some two weeks previously the C.E.G.B. had commenced delivery to the F.R. of the unsightly heaps of rails, chairs and miscellaneous track equipment which had been stacked in or near the flooded Tan-y-Grisiau Valley since the commencement of the project. There was good co-operation between the two bodies, with the result that some 400 lengths of rail, 500 fishplates and 3,700 chairs are now neatly stacked on a little-used part of the slate wharves at Minffordd. A smaller amount of similar material was delivered by British Railways from Blaenau at the same time. F.R. staff took on the responsibility for de-spiking and stacking the chairs—quite a substantial undertaking in itself; meanwhile volunteers thoroughly cleared the overgrown track along the edge of the wharf so that the newly-acquired stocks can be drawn upon when required. *Kidbrooke* has now been moved to the far end of this line, alongside Minffordd B.R. station, awaiting collection at its owner's convenience, and creates much interest and speculation among crews and passengers of passing trains.

It was on this newly-cleared length of track that the sixteen Alrewas four-wheeled Hudson ballast wagons first saw service, being loaded with sand and gravel by the "Tadpoles" on 24th August. This was for use in connection with the third stage of the erecting shop improvements, which embraces the concreting of the floor at the southern end. Other building work in hand at Boston Lodge includes the extension of the right-hand road in the carriage shed through into the old signal shop. In the erecting shop, work has started on the fabrication of a new steel frame for W.H.R. bogie coach No. 26.

Unlike last season when they were frequently required for locomotive repairs and operating duties, the permanent way staff have been able to concentrate on the track throughout the summer, and even managed to resleeper lengths of the main line between trains at Bryn Mawr and Minffordd, in addition to the routine maintenance which is so important during the peak season.

The Signals and Telegraph Department were very much in evidence during August Bank Holiday week, as usual. Work continued on the laying of the ten-core cable across the Cob, and test communication by this means was established at 5-30 p.m. on the Monday.

Yet another celebration took place during August, but this time the central figure was not *Prince* but fifteen-year-old Philip Mastin, from Chace Secondary Modern School, Enfield, the 500th "Tadpole" to take part in the regular holiday working parties organised from the school by Science Master Keith Catchpole. On the Friday evening, 23rd August, the twenty-five boys forming this season's party were received in grand style at the Town Hall, where Councillor Dr. W. Jones Morris, the Chairman of Portmadoc Urban Council, presented a silver cup to Philip, for the school, to mark the town's appreciation of the boys' work in helping to restore and maintain the Railway. The cup is to be awarded annually to the boy who performs his duties most satisfactorily as a member of a working party.

Next evening, the boys acted as hosts to the Councillors and their families, together with other guests, all of whom travelled to Tan-y-Bwlch in a special train behind *Prince*, driven, appropriately enough, by Mr. Catchpole. Coaches 12, 14 and 11 were used, giving a corridor buffet service throughout. The same train was used the following Friday, when the boys took their landladies for a ride. This was a severe test for the Railway's catering facilities, but fifty-six portions of fish and chips, followed by fruit flan, were served en route without a hitch.

In spite of all their engagements, the Tadpoles got through their usual mountain of work during their two weeks' visit. The main projects this time were the preparation of part of the erecting shop floor for concreting and the clearance of a cutting near Dduallt, both of which were tackled with their usual vigour and enthusiasm.

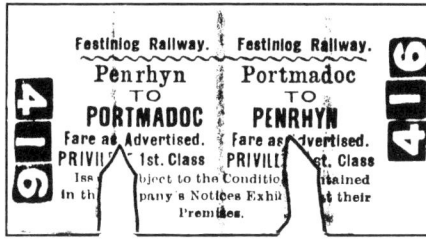

Festiniog Railway. Festiniog Railway.
Penrhyn Portmadoc
TO TO
PORTMADOC PENRHYN
Fare as Advertised. Fare as Advertised.
PRIVIL[1st. Class PRIVIL[st. Class
Iss[ ]bject to the Conditio[ ]tained
In th[ ]pany's Notices Exhi[ ]t their
Premises.

64. Penrhyn Quarries were abandoning their main line railway and so the FR was able to buy *Linda* as well as *Blanche*. The latter is seen cruising up Portmadoc High Street on 17th December. The PQR main line rail and chairs were also purchased. (A.G.W.Garraway)

1964

NEWS FROM THE LINE - Winter 1964

As the Centenary of Steam year draws to its close, we can look back with great satisfaction on another record season. With British Railways' figures still to come in (their accountants are involved with reorganisation following the inter-regional transfers), our final passenger journeys figure should be just under 130,000, an increase of 15,000 over 1962. It was another poor season for the North Wales tourist industry—the weather was particularly bad early in July when our traffic always needs a boost—and there is ample evidence that the increase was the result of our sustained publicity efforts.

There is little to report from the closing weeks of the season. Minor troubles were experienced with all three working locomotives; *Linda* continued to prove of great value and worked most of the end-of-season trains. Some specials were run during October, culminating with a double buffet car excursion on the 26th, in connection with the annual Staff Dinner, which collected the staff beforehand and took them home again afterwards. The next day the Gwynedd River Board took possession of the Cob to continue their strengthening work, which is involving the depositing of thousands of tons of rocks. Our telephone poles are being removed as they move across, having previously been stripped by the S. & T. department after the new cable had been put into commission.

The major item of locomotive news is the purchase, not only of *Linda*, but of her sister engine *Blanche* as well, from the Penrhyn Quarries. *Blanche* arrived at Minffordd by road on 17th December and will be given the same treatment as *Linda* as soon as practicable, to make her suitable for passenger train duties. Meanwhile, *Linda* has been stripped down for boiler examination and hydraulic test, to reveal a boiler barrel in a condition of pristine newness quite staggering for one of twenty-seven years' service—a pleasant change from what we have become rather accustomed to. Apart from a little work round the fire-box door ring, the boiler needs no attention, and reassembly with new lagging started at the end of November. The opportunity is being taken to make other minor repairs and adjustments, particularly to the motion to reduce the slack in the valve gear. Larger, hopper-type sand boxes are being fitted and, as a result of clearance tests in Garnedd tunnel, the cab roof is being re-profiled slightly. Her permanent tender is nearly completed and when attached, will increase her water capacity by about 150 gallons.

Prince needs little attention this winter, apart from the replacement of a rivet in the firehole door ring.

Merddin Emrys awaits some mechanical work as well as a small but very tricky fire-box repair; we have to face the fact that these fire-boxes are nearly worn out.

The overhaul of *Earl of Merioneth* continues, but slowly. Overhaul on the top-end bogie is nearly complete and work has been resumed on the other bogie, for which two new axle-boxes and many other components have been prepared. One pair of wheels, with sharp flanges, has had them built up to the correct profile by welding.

The Wickham trolley has had some repairs, with the fitment of new parts such as additional chain guards, and was handed back to a grateful Permanent Way Department on 1st December (with a consequent drop in the patronage of Crosville bus route R26).

After a short period of resleepering and general tidying up in the Highgate Crossing area at Penrhyn, the P.W. Dept. are now engaged in their main job for the winter: working up from Pen Cefn towards Rhiw Goch. With well over 100 lengths to be completely resleepered there is a great deal to do, but the work of screwing down has now been mechanised and good week-end working parties have been of assistance. All relaying is now being done by lifting the track clear of the old bed, levelling the ground and laying the new sleepers on top; ballast is then used properly for packing and filling in. With better quality sleepers on good ballast and chairs screwed down, the Festiniog track should be even finer than it has ever been and should remain good and strong for very many years. The section being relaid at present was the last bit of track relaid "on the cheap" in the winter of 1957-58, using poor quality sleepers and leaving quite a few of the old pre-war ones where possible. If the money had been available then, the track could have been relaid to the present standards almost as quickly; let us hope the days of patching up to get things running have gone for good, as it is more expensive in the long run.

A spare-time and very-wet-day job for the P.W. Dept. has been, and will be for many months to come, the redrilling of chairs to take the new galvanised screws. Eighty per cent of all chairs have at least one hole too small, due to faulty casting or the accumulation of rust and grime, and these have to be dealt with on the large drilling machine at Boston Lodge. Many of the 3,000 rectangular-based chairs brought down from Tan-y-Grisiau have been done (to the detriment of the meagre stock of 21/32 in. drills), but each day's relaying increases the stock awaiting attention by several dozen. As other patterns of chairs have extra large holes, the screw size had to be a compromise.

Another spare-time job tackled by certain members of the P.W. Dept. has been the thorough sorting out of the pattern loft. Anything of possible use has been carefully stored away, but many fascinating examples of the pattern-maker's art have been consigned to the archives or firewood pile, including items marked: "Snowdon Mountain Railway", "Welsh Highland Railway", "Votty & Bowydd Quarries" (locomotives *Taffy* and *Meirion*), "National Shell Factory" (Boston Lodge, first world war), and many other concerns, some of which seem to have no connection with the Festiniog Railway. The most interesting find is a pattern for a cast iron steam chest elbow identical to the one fabricated out of steel for *Merddin Emrys* last summer (see Magazine No. 22, page 7). The pattern is marked: "*Livingston Thompson*, 1920"; once more is demonstrated that few of our troubles are new ones!

Volunteers from Hants. and Sussex and London helped to complete the concreting of the floor at the west end of the erecting shop in October, which includes the provision of a fourth track primarily for the use of carriage body repairers. Electrical installations in the shop are being improved, and the wiring rationalised. Plans are being drawn up for the completion of the wheeldrop in the long shed by the provision of an overhead gantry.

With these, and many other improvements already made, Boston Lodge is rapidly becoming a relatively efficient and productive workshop far removed from the dinginess and chaos of eight years ago; it is certainly a busy works, and the staff have a great deal to do. From time to time complaints are received or overheard that visitors are not made welcome; this is far from true in the case of visitors who observe the customary formalities and obviously respect the fact that Boston Lodge is a railway works and not a working museum. It is not surprising, however, that people who just appear and wander around as if they own the place without so much as a word to anyone are regarded with a certain amount of suspicion.

Some years ago one of *Princess*'s number plates disappeared, several wagon plates have vanished and now, this summer, one of the Peckett's works plates has been removed from the side of the cab (the other has since been removed to a safer place). We know that name and number plates from scrapped engines are getting increasingly difficult to come by, but when people resort to stealing them from vehicles in use or locomotives in store awaiting rebuilding is it any wonder that visitors to Boston Lodge may be treated a little suspiciously? The depths to which some fanatics will go to get souvenirs these days is abysmally low; such an "exhibit" will surely lose much of its appeal by virtue of its "hot" nature. We doubt whether Society members are involved, but if any should come across it we trust they will do their best to see that it is returned to Portmadoc—perhaps in an anonymous parcel like one of *Prince*'s old name plates.

We have recently been pleased to receive back one of *Little Giant*'s bells. This has been very kindly donated by Greaves Quarries in memory of R. M. Greaves, of Wern, one-time Chairman of the Festiniog Railway Company. Latterly it has served as the incline warning bell at the top of the incline from Dinas to Llechwedd Quarry.

65. Glan-y-Mor Yard was used for storage of PW materials but this activity was later concentrated at Minffordd Yard. This crane had been used for unloading and stacking timber for shipbuilding. It was sawn in the FR sawmill prior to sale to shipbuilders, quarry owners etc. (A.G.W.Garraway)

66. One of the achievements in March was the relaying of the three-way stub points at the lowest end of the railway and replacing it with two orthodox turnouts. The old points were reused in Glan-y-Mor Yard. Note that part of the level crossing was still in place at that time. (A.G.W.Garraway)

67.   The Royal Engineers undertook an exercise on the FR in April and moved their crane to Glan-y-Mor yard to set about erecting the steelwork for the carriage shed extension. This was a much needed facility as many of the vehicles restored earlier were deteriorating faster than they could be maintained. (A.G.W.Garraway)

68.   The exercise was known as "Operation Little Giant" and initially involved driving the crane from Portmadoc astride the track on the Cob. It was to be many years before there was road access to the Works. The finished framework can be seen in picture no. 94. (A.G.W.Garraway)

69. During the erection work, *Moelwyn* broke its driving axle. The ever resourceful REs simply picked the locomotive up and left the drunken wheelset sprawling on the track. (A.G.W.Garraway)

NEWS FROM THE LINE - Spring 1964

Beginning, as usual, with the locomotive situation, we find *Earl of Merioneth* and *Linda* still occupying the main berths in the erecting shop. Some slow progress has been made with the Fairlie, including the preparation of new side rods and big end brasses. *Linda*'s reprofiled cab is back in position and she is now being fitted with steam brake for the engine, using a brake cylinder borrowed from the Peckett, with a Mark VI graduable steam brake valve. Some front end improvements have been made, and she is being equipped with a concrete arch. The cab reprofiling has been done thoughtfully (perhaps with *Russell* in mind), and we are confident that everyone will agree that her looks have been definitely improved. Her repaint in Festiniog green livery is nearing completion.

Merddin Emrys and *Prince* are both more or less ready for service, the latter having been retubed. *Blanche* is tucked away in the locomotive shed, her wheels having been sent away to Leeds for adjustment. *Moelwyn* fractured a flycrank early in January; a temporary repair has now been effected while a new one is being made, but in the meantime the Simplex has seen a good deal of service on works and permanent way shunting duties. The Hudson/Hunslet diesel, which was acquired by the White Rose Group in October, 1962, and has since been extensively overhauled in Leeds, arrived on 9th March, looking very smart and named *Tyke*.

Buffet Car No. 14 is being re-equipped with roller bearings, kindly provided by Skefko at a very special price. All coaches have had their axle boxes checked and various improvements have been made to the bodywork of several; No. 15 has been reroofed in ply and No. 11's roof has been refelted. A programme of new coach construction is now in progress; the profile will be similar to No. 14, and it is hoped that the first one will be in service this summer.

A major improvement is now in hand at Boston Lodge. A second-hand building has been purchased from Leeds, which fits neatly into the space in front of the Glan-y-Mor carriage shed. It will form a continuation, not only of that building, but also of the erecting shop and thus there will be a large L-shaped continuously covered area from the machine shop round to the rear of Glan-y-Mor, with accommodation for four more bogie coaches and plenty of scope for further improvements. The metalwork of the building has already started to arrive, and arrangements have been made for the Royal Engineers to give some valuable assistance in its erection as a training project.

At the beginning of February, two wagons of wood-working machinery and welding equipment, as well as Pullman seating and many other useful items, arrived at Minffordd from the former Pullman Company's works at Preston Park, purchased on its closure.

On the track, the relaying at Rhiw Goch is completed except for the topping-up of ballast. Short sections at Tylers, Hafod-y-Llyn and Minffordd all need attention before the main summer service starts, and some work will be required on the Cob now the River Board have finished. Some twenty-four B.R. wagons of ballast were received at Minffordd soon after Christmas, and relaying had to stop for more than two weeks while they were unloaded. It was a problem to find sufficient F.R. wagons for ballast in such quantity. During evening shifts at Boston Lodge, slate wagons were fitted with wooden sides, crudely manufactured from the old erecting shop flooring, other wagons awaiting repair were pressed into service, and anything movable that would hold ballast was borrowed from other departments. At one stage more than forty vehicles were standing loaded in the sidings at Minffordd, but very many tons of ballast were needed for the relaying at Rhiw Goch and elsewhere, and the stocks are now down to more reasonable proportions. There should still be plenty of ballasting work available for keen volunteers on non-traffic evenings during the summer.

Volunteers, particularly the consistent fortnightly parties from London, have played an important part in the relaying programme. Their main tasks have been the removal of turf and weeds from the lengths to be relaid and the clearance of old sleepers, chairs and spikes from the site after relaying. Now that chairs have to be drilled at Boston Lodge before being used, extra time has to be spent man-handling them on the site, and it is fortunate that volunteers have been on hand for this work. Mention must also be made of a rather special working party on 4th January. In addition to the usual party from London and the tail end of the annual New Year party from Cambridge University, we had the pleasure of a visit from a dozen members of the North Western Area of the T.R.P.S. Mr. J. I. C. Boyd was among their number, and he has sent us two photographs of their ballasting activities, one of which we are pleased to publish to illustrate these notes.

Plans are in hand for the redevelopment of the South Snowdon Wharf at Portmadoc, including the building of holiday flatlets. Such development is obviously very desirable, and the Railway should certainly benefit. Road access to the wharf at present leads past the end of Harbour Station and crosses the line near the three-way stub point, but with road traffic bound to increase, this arrangement is considered unsatisfactory and the crossing is to be abolished. Instead, the road will skirt round the end of our line, and to make way for it some realignment of the pointwork and engine spur is being made and will be completed before the start of the season. The stub point has been carefully dismantled, not being suitable for the new layout, and will be used in a less busy location in due course.

70. The Hudson Hunslet diesel *Tyke* arrived on 9th March after a long overhaul by the White Rose Group. It ran a total of 180 miles on the FR, much of it in connection with a GPO cable laying contract on the Cob in 1966. It was dismantled in 1979. The Simplex carried the name *Mary-Ann* from about 1963 but lost the hyphen later. (A.G.W.Garraway)

The FR announced in March its intention to build a deviation on the east side of the lake that was blocking its route, but ultimately it was constructed on the west side. A journey along the top of the dam would have been an added attraction.

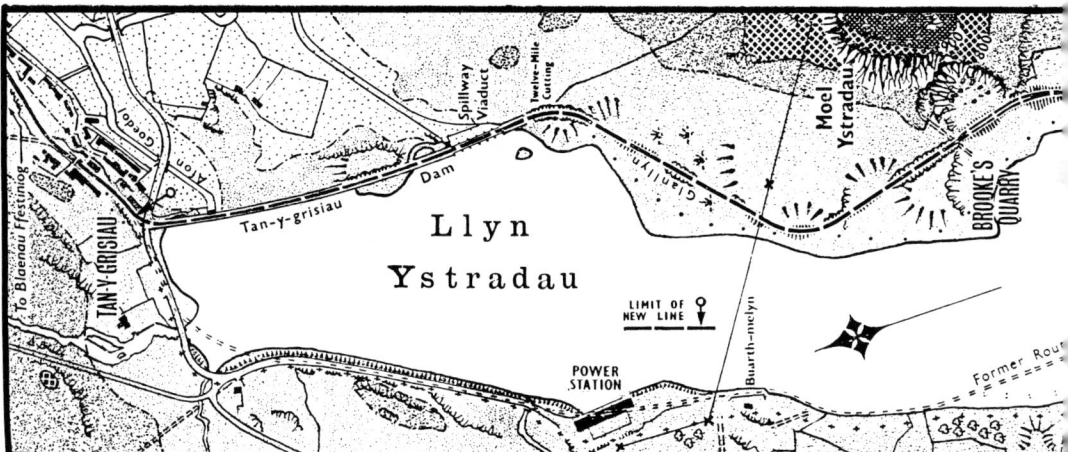

71. *Linda* ran as an 0-4-0ST until fitted with a pony truck in 1969. Initially she ran on the FR attached to an old England tender, as seen in picture no. 63, but parts from another England tender were used to make a new one with water and coal space. The cab was modified and the whole repainted in FR livery, as seen in April. (A.G.W.Garraway)

(D.H.Wilson)

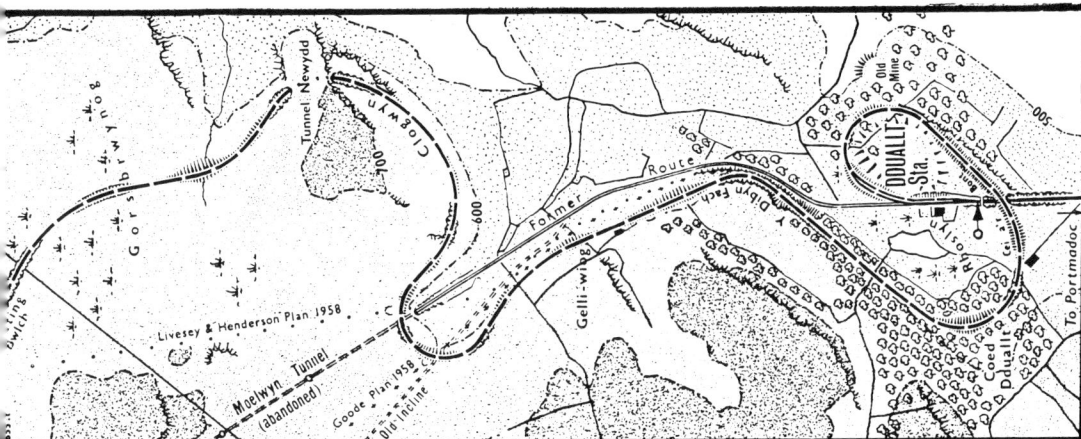

The Llyn Ystradau Deviation. Scale: six inches to the mile. The ruling gradient is 1 in 80, compensated to 1 in 100 on sharp curves (minimum radius 180 feet at Tan-y-Grisiau) with level stretches on the dam and at Brooke's Quarry and a 1 in 140 climb from the latter to the summit. The dotted and crossed routes are earlier, rejected ones involving long tunnels.

Deviation announced

The Festiniog Railway have now announced the new route by which it is proposed to restore the line between Dduallt and Tan-y-Grisiau. The track which had been in use since 1844 was compulsorily acquired in June, 1956, for the construction of the lower reservoir of the pumped storage scheme. It was originally envisaged that the new route would go to the west of the reservoir passing close to the power station and a detail survey of this route was completed in 1957 by Mr. A. R. Goode, M.I.C.E. Unfortunately, however, there is not enough space between the power station and the hillside for this comparatively simple solution. A second survey, completed in 1958 by Messrs. Livesey & Henderson, consulting engineers to the Festiniog Railway, envisaged a new tunnel of 620 yards to the east shore of the reservoir and a viaduct over the spillway of the dam, along which the line would regain its old route at Tan-y-Grisiau. This second route would have cost more than double the cost of the west side route.

A third survey has now been completed by Mr. Gerald Fox with the help of nearly fifty volunteers, and has been checked and approved by Messrs. Livesey & Henderson. The resulting proposals, by reducing the length of tunnel to seventy-five yards, are calculated to reduce the cost of construction considerably. In order to achieve this, the line is to be carried to a summit of 655 feet on the top of the high ridge between Moelwyn and Moel Ystradau, gaining some of the height by taking a spiral round a small hill to the east of Dduallt station, gradients being no steeper than the ruling Festiniog gradient of 1 in 80 which is compensated on the numerous curves. On the spiral, and on a horseshoe curve where the line curves through more than 180 degrees, the radius of the curves will be 200 feet and 215 feet respectively with the gradient eased to 1 in 100. These curves are, however, not as sharp as Tyler's Curve, below Tan-y-Bwlch, which has a radius of about 115 feet. North of the ridge the line will cross the level of Brookes Quarry and descend at 1 in 80 to the dam by which it will cross to Tan-y-Grisiau, where it will rejoin the old route.

This new route will complete the passenger railway link between Portmadoc and Blaenau Ffestiniog, and thus between the North Wales and Cambrian Coast resorts. It will bring to fruition the efforts of many hundreds of volunteers, particularly members of the Festiniog Railway Society who are now calculated to have spent over 300,000 man-hours of voluntary work on restoring the Festiniog Railway. It will also provide a unique opportunity for the public to view the pumped storage scheme, the Power House and the Llyn Stwlan dam being seen to their best advantage across the waters of Llyn Ystradau. This exceptionally fine view of the first pumped storage scheme would not otherwise be possible for the public.

GORSBRWYNOG from above tunnel

72. No. 1 van was built by the Midland Group and was delivered on 27th June. The wheels, bearings and other components were from a dismantled quarrymen's coach. The old no. 1 van's body was grounded at Dduallt. (A.G.W.Garraway)

73. With the ever increasing traffic, together with the difficulty of repairing the old coaches left out of doors, it was decided to embark on a programme of building new coaches. The parts were prefabricated by a joinery firm in Birkenhead and then assembled, as seen here at Boston Lodge. (A.G.W.Garraway)

74. No. 24 (soon renumbered 104) presented some bogie clearance problem on its first test trip over the sharp curves of Harbour station on 24th June. The first class saloon was fitted with ex-Pullman car seats. (A.G.W.Garraway)

75. When *Blanche* arrived she was modified to run with wagon no. 38 (earlier used by *Linda*) and is seen returning from Tan-y-bwlch after working her first up train. *Linda* is waiting to proceed on 24th June. (A.G.W.Garraway)

NEWS FROM THE LINE - Summer 1964

The 1964 operating season got off to an encouraging start, with the passenger figures for Easter comparing well with last year's in spite of the earlier date. *Linda* handled most of the traffic, and her smart appearance earned many admiring comments from passengers. With a couple of bogie coaches undergoing minor adjustments in the works and the weather not being warm enough to use the open Welsh Highlands, it was decided to bring out the four-wheelers on Easter Sunday—an unusual sight so early in the season. *Linda* handled the train of six bogies and five four-wheelers with ease.

Things quietened down after the bank holiday, but traffic on the daily train throughout the Easter school holidays was sufficient to show that we may have lost some trade in previous years by only running a weekly train in this period. Whit week brought good crowds, but with a five-train service (Monday to Friday) being shown in the timetable there was no likelihood of a repeat of last year's sensational ten-coacher. The heaviest train was on Whit Sunday, when *Linda* and *Prince* double-headed a train of eight bogies. Later in the week there was a welcome tendency for the morning train to be well filled, and on 20th May *Prince* (and Bill Hoole) surprised everyone by keeping perfect time on the 10-45 with six bogies, a hefty load for the veteran but proof that the roller bearings fitted to buffet car No. 14 have made a real difference to the free running of that vehicle. Now that the coaches are properly run in again it is being found that, as a result of this modification, each engine can handle a train with one coach more than it would have been trusted with last year with No. 14 in the formation.

The National Urdd (Youth) Eisteddfod was held in Portmadoc at the end of Whit week and was reputed to have brought some 20,000 visitors to the town, but in spite of publicity on both Welsh TV channels the Railway did not seem to benefit to any marked extent. However, on the Friday, traffic was boosted by a party of schoolchildren from Flintshire who travelled on the line under a schools educational scheme. Two hundred travelled up, and a further 200 down, on the midday train, retimed to permit the main-train set to be used. *Merddin Emrys* and *Prince* double-headed the eight-bogie train. Further schools are visiting the line under similar arrangements during the summer.

With more engines available, the ideal of regular manning has at last become completely possible. The Manager continues to run *Linda* (as he has done since her arrival) and Evan Davies handles *Merddin Emrys* so that one of the mechanical staff can give the skilled attention so desirable for these machines. Bill Hoole will take charge of *Blanche* as soon as she is ready for service, whilst *Prince* will be kept as spare and stand-by engine. The old pre-Grouping practice of exhibiting the driver's name in the locomotive's cab has been adopted. *Linda* now boasts a second whistle—ex a Great Central Railway "Pom Pom" Class J.11; not quite up to A.4 standard, perhaps, but better than nothing.

With three steam engines in good shape and a fourth almost ready to enter service, there is little concern over the fact that our "modern power" fleet is somewhat depleted. *Moelwyn* and the Simplex have both been out of action for some weeks with various mechanical defects, but should soon be back at work. *Tyke* is proving a useful machine, within severe speed limitations and, apart from being rather tiresome to start, makes an ideal works shunter.

The most important recent development from Boston Lodge was only mentioned very briefly in the last Magazine, and can now be dealt with in greater detail. This, of course, concerns the building of new coaches. Extension of track mileage calls for additional coaching stock to meet peak loads and increased traffic potential, and it has been decided to build several new coaches at Boston Lodge to the general external design of No. 14. The first off the production line, No. 24, is to be a fairly straightforward saloon coach, with thirty-two third-class seats and four firsts. It will have a sixteen-seat third-class saloon at each end, each having a door on either side, and a small first-class saloon in the centre with four ex-Pullman car seats but no external doors. The bodywork was built in Birkenhead during the winter and was delivered to Boston Lodge in sections early in March. The fabrication of the chassis was unfortunately delayed, but work proceeded throughout April and assembly of the bodywork on the frame was completed in May. Much work remains to be done on the roof, interior fittings, brake gear, etc., but it is expected that the coach will be in service by August. If all goes well it is to be fitted with bogies ex luggage brake van No. 3 (old series); this was broken up many years ago, but the bogies were retained and have now been sent to the Midland Group's C. & W. Department for reconditioning.

The intention is that one new coach should be tackled each year, but as the result of an anonymous donation of £1,500 which has been allocated to the second vehicle the ordering of material has been brought forward and construction of the underframe has already begun. This is to be a first-class observation car/dining saloon/brake and it should be in service by next Easter. We shall therefore begin our passenger-carrying centenary year with a rake of three new-pattern corridor-connected coaches (observation/buffet/saloon) for the main train, and the old-pattern Nos. 11 and 12 (observation/buffet) for the second train, both sets having ample guard's and luggage accommodation. In addition to giving increased passenger accommodation and revenue, the new coaches should help to increase operating efficiency.

The framework of the new building at Boston Lodge, described in the last Magazine, was erected in March by 483 Port Maintenance Troop, Royal Engineers, as their exercise "Little Giant". The twenty-three man party camped near Boston Lodge for just on three weeks, using buffet No. 14 as their canteen. They brought their own mobile crane, which had to be driven over the Cob to gain access to the works yard, and a four-wheeled Michigan shovel, nicknamed *Leaping Lulu*, which was used to clear and roughly level a badly overgrown portion of Glan-y-Mor yard, as well as to prepare the building site. The long road in the locomotive shed will in due course be extended into this new building, giving a sunken road which will be very useful for work on the roofs and upperworks of vehicles.

At the same time, contractors for the developers were working on the alterations to the track layout at the south end of Harbour Station. Work is not starting on the actual development of South Snowdon Wharf until the autumn, but the alterations to our layout were the first requirement for the provision of good road access to the site. Furthermore, it was essential that this work was completed early, so that the three-way stub point could be incorporated in the alterations to be made in Glan-y-Mor yard this summer.

On the permanent way, sections at Pen Cefn and Cemetery Cutting have been resleepered since Easter, and work has started on the stretch from Whistling Curve to Tan-y-Bwlch Bridge. In order to get possession of the track for as long as possible, the p.w. gang are working from 6-0 a.m. to 2-0 p.m. on Saturdays and Sundays. The adoption of new standards of relaying, involving the lifting of the track level and consequently eliminating the digging-out process, has meant that more voluntary labour has been available for other jobs in the past few months. As a result, there has been quite a remarkable improvement in the general appearance of the track.

In the forestry area, clearance along both sides of the track should help to reduce the risk of fire; track drainage has benefited from the increased attention to all major cesses and ditches, and in Whit week the "Tadpoles" cut down hundreds of bushes in a brave attempt to improve the view from the line between Milestone Curve and Tylers, as well as having their annual onslaught on encroaching vegetation generally. Drainage work has continued on the Tan-y-Bwlch/Dduallt section, and this essential first step to the relaying programme should be completed soon.

Siding accommodation is an ever-present problem at Boston Lodge and Minffordd, and with more labour available steps can at last be taken to improve the position. A site has been cleared at Minffordd for a badly-needed shunting siding in the fork between the long siding (alongside the main line) and the steeply-graded curving line down into the exchange sidings. This will greatly speed up the shunting of wagons out of the long siding, particularly in wet weather when there is a severe limit to the number of loaded wagons which can conveniently be parked on the steeply-graded line. Other, more long term, developments here are being considered. At Boston Lodge, clearance started at Easter outside the carriage shed, with a view to the realignment of the roads leading into that shed. This will give a straight entry through the doors instead of the present very treacherous curve and will facilitate the rebuilding of the third road shed in lean-to form. Here, too, more ambitious plans are at an embryo stage. Perhaps the most notable development is at Glan-y-Mor, where sidings are to be laid on the site cleared by the Royal Engineers and the present ash siding (erstwhile Glan-y-Mor and Port Meirion Extension Railway) is to be extended in the general direction of Port Meirion. The three-way stub point from Harbour Station is being incorporated in the new layout.

76. The Wickham trolley, seen earlier in picture 50, was finished during the Summer. It proved useful, running over 2000 miles in some years, but was little used after 1969. (A.G.W.Garraway)

NEWS FROM THE LINE - Autumn 1964

It is a pleasure to be able to report on another successful operating season— at least up to the close of the peak service timetable. Thanks to the availability of four steam locomotives and additional coaching stock, all departments have run efficiently and smoothly, and an increased number of passengers has been carried in greater comfort.

Neither individual days nor weeks have reached the peaks of last year; one or two weeks have actually been down on the corresponding weeks of 1963, but this would seem due to the inevitable small peaks and troughs in the "graph" being a week different this year. The best week of the summer was the fourth in August, which became the second busiest ever with 12,103 passenger journeys, the record having been set in the third week of August last year with 12,571. Earlier, the last week in July had produced just over 11,000—the first time the 10,000 mark has been reached in July.

At the end of the full summer service on September 5th, the number of journeys had reached the total for last year. Although the September/October results in total are far less than an average August week, they will give us the season's increase.

All these figures are based on tickets issued on the Railway, and do not include traffic from B.R. and coach firm inclusive tours, the detailed results for which are not known until the end of the season. Some, we know, are well up on last year, and we have one or two new tours, so there is every hope that they also will show an increase.

A feature of the year has been the ease with which peak traffic has been carried. Rarely have guards had to resort to packing-in tactics and only on a couple of occasions have TRAIN FULL notices been exhibited. One of the reasons for this has been the popularity of the evening train, and it is pleasing to note that Society members have been making an obvious effort to travel on this train rather than add to possible congestion on the afternoon trains. Sunday travel has been as popular as ever, and, in order to spread the load and avoid what could be embarrassingly long trains in wet weather, two trains have been run on August Sundays, leaving Portmadoc at 2-20 and 3-00 p.m., the first departing from Tan-y-Bwlch on arrival of the second at 3-40.

By contrast, the Saturday morning train, as always, has been very poorly patronised. The first of the season, on July 25th, produced such a small complement of passengers that the guard reduced the train to two coaches—11 and 14—and they were half empty. Prince's crew didn't seem to mind the indignity of it, and during the journey the buffet car attendant was able to serve them with their "elevenses" through the connecting door of No. 14—an operation which greatly amused the passengers.

Throughout the season the motive power situation has been adequate. With regularly manned engines each only working two trips daily with reasonable lay-overs between, the trains have been handled with ease; in fact, lost time (usually due to waiting B.R. connections) has often been regained, and late arrivals, even of only a minute or two, have been very infrequent. Crews have had time to clean fires ready for each trip, and tube cleaning and general maintenance has been done regularly. The coal bill has again gone up, but efficient working and heavier trains are bound to result in an increase in this respect—and are offset by more satisfied customers.

As trains got heavier, Prince retired from the weekday service, apart from evening trains, but was often to be seen at Minffordd on coal and works train shunting duties. Normally, Merddin Emrys worked the 11-45 and 2-15 departures, Blanche the 10-30 and 3-00 and Linda the 1-00 and 4-30. The main train set, with the observation car and Snapper Bar, ran on the 11-45, 2-15 and 4-30, with four other bogies and the four-wheelers. When the new saloon coach entered service on August 25th it was added to the formation, first in front of No. 14 then between 14 and 11 as guard and buffet car attendants found how they could make best use of the corridor connections. The four-wheelers were then transferred to the "B" train, in exchange for a W.H.R. bogie.

An advantage of having a fresh engine for each trip has been the avoidance of delays caused by shunting during short turn-round periods, particularly between 4-15 and 4-30. Often, however, traffic requirements have not permitted Linda to lighten her load and she has had to take the full load of six bogies and six four-wheelers or, on one occasion at the end of August, eight bogies. On that trip she regained two minutes, with a stop at Penrhyn; it involved working with practically full regulator—130 lbs. steam-chest pressure on a 140 lbs. engine—and about fifty per cent cut off, not bad going for a 71-year-old slide valve wet steam engine!

There was an adjustment to the regular manning roster, as given in the last magazine. It was found that *Prince's* duties would keep Bill Hoole sufficiently occupied, and David Baskcomb therefore has driven *Blanche* throughout the season.

The only delay due to mechanical failure during the summer season involved the 10-30 up towards the end of July, when a failure on coach No. 17 made it impossible to release the brakes with vacuum when restarting from Penrhyn. A call was put through to Boston Lodge while the coach was being detached from the train and shunted into the loop. Fitters came up by car and effected complete repairs so that the train was able to pick up its coach again on the down journey; a smart bit of work which was hampered by the high level of the ballast—wriggling under the coach being a most difficult operation.

The summer has been quite a productive one for the permanent way department. Much time has, of course, been devoted to the routine maintenance so essential when traffic is heavy, but there is also more concrete evidence of hard work by both staff and volunteers in the form of relaid main line and newly-laid sidings. By working from 6-00 a.m. to 2-00 p.m. on Saturdays and Sundays during June and July, the P.W. gang were able to resleeper from Hafod-y-Llyn to Tan-y-Bwlch Bridge. They then turned their attention to the new layout at Glan-y-Mor, where the three-way stub points were laid in as planned and the old fourth road siding completely relaid. At the time of writing, the fifth road is taking shape, being a completely new siding leading round past the old gunpowder sheds. The old fifth road, of useless light "T" section rail, was taken out after *Palmerston* and the derelict four-wheeled coach had been coaxed on to the new track.

Work has also been done at Tan-y-Bwlch, with the two-fold object of increasing car-parking space and providing suitable siding accommodation for the permanent way work which will undoubtedly be based there at some time in the future. All the old sidings were taken out; (as a measure of their uselessness, not a single sleeper was encountered, apart from one or two under

the points), and the rails used for a completely new siding as close to the main line as practicable. A good deal of tree lopping and ditch clearance was also done, and efforts made to improve the appearance of the station generally.

The bulging drystone wall above Penrhyn Crossing has been taken down and rebuilt entirely by volunteer labour, and looks a professional job. Work has also started on rebuilding the parapet wall on Cei Mawr, and a fencing section from the Lancs. & Cheshire Group has done some useful repairs. Volunteers have also prepared and erected many notices warning people not to walk along the track. Thus results are beginning to be seen from the repeated requests for people who can do walling and fencing, but there is still a tremendous amount to be done.

The increase in traffic coupled with the improvement in the motive power position, enabling longer trains to be run, has introduced its own problems; nine coach trains have been found practicable—and roller bearings on the new stock may make for more—but six bogies, six four-wheelers and a double engine only just fit in clear on the loop at Minffordd. Work has therefore started on clearing trees and bushes and preparing the ground at the east end of Minffordd Station in readiness for the lengthening of the loop during the winter. The same problem is present at Portmadoc, but a little slewing of the tracks during July enabled fuller use to be made of the loops there without risk of scraping coach sides. However, very soon the *Princess*-style buffer stops will have to move westwards.

All the projects tackled so far have depended a good deal on volunteer labour, and it is thanks to the good turn-out of both individuals and organised parties that so much has been accomplished. Towards the end of August there were parties from Chace School, Enfield, (the "Tadpoles"), Brambleton Model Railway Club, Harpenden, Lancs. and Cheshire and London Groups, as well as numerous individuals. The Tadpoles' main job was in connection with the laying of vast amounts of concrete at Boston Lodge, with the result that the long task of concreting the erecting shop/machine shop floor has now been successfully completed. This work has been carried out during the Tadpoles' visits over four summers, under Fred Boughey's general guidance, with John Andrews acting as chargeman in the last couple of years.

1965

77. A completely new tender was constructed for *Blanche*. It was altogether slightly larger than that for *Linda* and the tender cab gave a more comfortable downhill run in inclement weather. (A.G.W.Garraway)

78. Once the first part of the Deviation route had been determined and the first piece of land to form the spiral given to the railway, digging started by hand on 1st January. The photograph was taken two days later. (A.G.W.Garraway)

NEWS FROM THE LINE - Winter 1965

The consistent increase in passenger figures noted in the off-peak months of June and July was maintained throughout the period of the Autumn time-table. Many unscheduled trains were run, particularly during the mornings on days when only afternoon trains were shown on the time-table; in spite of the very limited publicity that could be given for such trains they were always worthwhile and some carried forty or fifty passengers. The final passenger journey figure for the year is just over 144,000.

Linda handled most of the traffic towards the end of the season, with *Prince* standing in occasionally, the service running with almost monotonous precision. Not even a seven coach load on a wet rail gave *Linda* any trouble, thanks to the use of dry sand, and *Prince* took six on one occasion.

The second from last week of the operating season gave an opportunity for the Narrow-Gauge Fraternity to get together again. Several old friends visited the Festiniog on October 7th, and the following day all members of the F.R. staff (except Evie Roberts, regrettably unfit), wives, and other Company and Society officials travelled to Aberystwyth (mostly via the Cambrian Coast Express) where they were joined by representatives of the Talyllyn, Fairbourne, W. & L., R. & E. and R.H. & D. Railways. Lunch was taken at the King's Hall, where Mr. Philip Davies, Clerk of Aberystwyth Town Council, and Mr. Oliver Veltom, of British Railways, gave a warm welcome, then the gathering made their way to the station, where *Llywelyn* was waiting with a specially chartered train which included a special van for Alan Skellern's scooter. In spite of unpleasant weather, the return trip to Devil's Bridge was enjoyed by all, and made a welcome change of scenery for those who had been heavily engaged in the operation of the various privately-operated narrow-gauge lines during the summer.

Back on the Festiniog, the autumn work programme was getting under way, with Boston Lodge paying particular attention to the running gear and drawgear of coaches. Trouble has been experienced with broken bolster springs on the bogies of the heavier coaches, and to get over this a Mark 2 bolster design has been prepared which can take heavier springs. No. 24 had the first bogies of this pattern and these have now been put under No. 15,

which is our heaviest vehicle when fully loaded. Those taken from 15 will be used for No. 26, the bogies from which only have the original experimental bolster arrangement. No. 26, a Welsh Highland coach, has had its wooden underwork removed, and will have been mounted on its new steel under-frame by the time these notes appear in print. The bodywork of the observation car, No. 100, arrived early in October and has now been assembled on its frame.

Several coaches have been weighed at Minffordd, and it is hoped to have tare weights painted on them in due course for the benefit of locomotive performance addicts and others.

The bodywork of No. 100 was brought to Boston Lodge from our sub-contractors in Birkenhead early in October on the Festiniog Railway Company's lorry (*first mentioned in the White Rose Group notes, Magazine No. 25*). Stalwarts of the Group have been overhauling the lorry in Leeds; the body-work has claimed most of their attention as the vehicle is in good mechanical order and takes the road every few weeks on a trip to Portmadoc. The first visit was at the end of August, with a powered radial drilling machine, ex Manchester, for the machine shop at Boston Lodge.

October, as usual, was an interesting month in the permanent way depart-ment, providing an opportunity to dispose of various small and sometimes unusual jobs, with possession of the track if necessary, before the main part of the winter's relaying programme was tackled. The chief project was the lengthening of the eastern end of Minffordd loop by seven lengths. After preparatory work had been completed, the points were jacked up and towed bodily by *Moelwyn* along the top of the track to their new location, while the displaced sleepers and rails were used to fill the gap vacated by the points. Some slight adjustment of the rails in between was necessary, after which the main line connection was restored and *Moelwyn* was able to return to the works the same day. The completion of the loop still involved quite a lot of work, and *Moelwyn* was again used to pull down a large poplar tree of eight foot girth which was in the way. Unfortunately, nobody remembered to prop up the roots while the trunk was being cut up, and after a number of slices had been cut several tons of stump toppled back into the hole, necessitating yet another visit by the diesel. After this it was a straightforward job laying in the additional track, aligning the old and new lines and completing the point lever mechanism.

The completion of the new fifth road in Glan-y-Mor yard round past the gunpowder sheds was left over for next summer, but a new job started in September was the lowering of the left-hand track in Glan-y-Mor paint shop. The low roof of this building has always given trouble, and as the standard profile of the new coaches makes full use of every inch of the loading gauge something had to be done. Unfortunately, the track is laid on very solid rock and the job has had to be held up until a compressor with rock-breaking equipment could be borrowed. This arrived in Mid-November and the job was finished as soon as possible afterwards.

Earlier that month the gang had spent a week on the Tan-y-Bwlch-Dduallt section, putting in new keys and replacing a hundred or so of the worst, largely non-existent, sleepers, so that works trains can continue to be run over the section.

The first straightforward relaying job of the winter involved the section from Lloc Meurig crossing, just above the Cemetery, to the point adjacent to the start of the long siding at Minffordd. This was due to be followed by the crossing and cutting below Penrhyn and by the completion of the long length from Whistling Curve to Tan-y-Bwlch bridge.

The P.W. Dept. are also involved in big developments in hand at Minffordd exchange sidings. The goods shed, which has been leased out as a saw-mill since about 1940, has been vacated by the tenants and the large well-built corrugated iron building behind it has also been acquired by the Railway Company. The standard-gauge line into the goods shed is in good shape now vast quantities of sawdust have been removed, and is being used for incoming traffic; 300 sleepers have been unloaded in there, and also 12,000 wood keys recently purchased from B.R. Eventually, sleepers will be cut and then loaded on to F.R. vehicles all under the same roof, but there are matters such as the installation of electricity and the restoration of the F.R. connection into the building to be tackled first. The other building will be used for other p.w. activities, such as chair drilling and key creosoting, and could be used for more ambitious work such as the sub-assembly of sleepers and chairs should bad weather drive the gang under cover for any length of time, as it did in the winter of 1963. There are also plans under discussion to make use of the old Llechwedd slate wharf and the crane thereon. The only line leading to this wharf passes through the goods shed, and the wharf has therefore been disused and overgrown for many years, probably since well before the last war.

A project recently tackled jointly by the Works and P.W. Departments has been the complete rebuilding of the coal/ballast chute. The old chute, together with quite a lot of the wall supporting it, was demolished, and a new concrete structure built up, with separate coal chute and ballast grid side by side. The two tracks underneath will have to be slewed and relaid before the chutes can be used to best effect; in the meantime ballast is being transhipped on the main slate wharf.

79. The Penrhyn Quarry Railway main line was laid with bull head rail of similar section to that which had been the last to be acquired by the FR, though of only 24ft in length against the 30ft of the FR. It provided a much needed stock of rails and chairs. It was lifted and transported to Minffordd. A typical slate slab fencing can also be seen. (A.G.W.Garraway)

80. For the new coaches, fresh bogies were constructed of longer wheelbase similar to those on the Lynton & Barnstaple coach. They had improved suspension with roller bearings, Metalastik primary suspension and dampers on the secondary springs. This bogie is for no. 100 and has swing links, whereas those for no. 24 had plain bolsters. (A.G.W.Garraway)

81. Known as the "Bunny Hutch", this building at Tan-y-bwlch served as both booking office and souvenir shop. The recently retired BR platform ticket machine would issue an unnecessary ticket for two old pennies. (A.G.W.Garraway)

82. As part of the efforts to improve the standard of the track, a member borrowed a Hallade track recorder to analyse the track condition from the train. The instrument recorded level, alignment and super-elevation. (A.G.W.Garraway)

83. One of the design weaknesses of *Linda* and *Blanche* was that their large and powerful cylinders were mounted very high above the frames. Those on *Blanche* had cracked and worked loose. The right side block is seen upside down after removal. (A.G.W.Garraway)

84. Here we see the temporary track used to take the material being dug and to make the embankment at the north end of Dduallt.

Many of the volunteer "Deviationists" were undergraduates at Cambridge University. (A.G.W.Garraway)

85. In any railway construction, the aim is always to make the amount dug from the cutting provide the amount needed for the embankment. The Hudson tipper wagons were from a gravel pit near Chichester, West Sussex, and were renovated by the Hants & Sussex Area Group. (A.G.W.Garraway)

NEWS FROM THE LINE - Spring 1965

Boston Lodge

We will begin with news of coaches, not only to conform to the theme of this Passenger Centenary year, but also because a very considerable amount of work has been devoted to coaching stock in Boston Lodge in recent months. The most notable development has been the building of bogies in the erecting shop; twelve flame-cut sidemembers arrived just before Christmas, and work started on the fabrication of the first pair—for coach No. 24—as soon as floor-space was available.

They are being built to the same wheelbase as the Lynton & Barnstaple bogies—4 ft. 4 ins.—and with the brake gear inside the wheels, so that they are no longer, overall, than standard Festiniog bogies and therefore fully interchangeable. Roller bearing axleboxes are standard equipment. Traffic having now reached the stage of 100 years ago in that on certain days in August the line is working to maximum capacity and there is no possibility of fitting more trains into the schedule, ways have to be found of carrying more passengers, in comfort, per train. Experience with the fitting of the SKF bearings to No. 14 has indicated that this is one way of enabling the existing engines to haul more coaches, so through the kind help of Mr. Thompson and the Skefko authorities, we are being provided with sets of new roller bearing axleboxes, and, furthermore, Mr. Thompson has inveigled Metalastik Ltd. to supply appropriate units for rubber suspension at a very attractive price.

The use of Metalastik primary suspension avoids the accurate machining and fitting of horn guides, and simplifies construction considerably. The design has been prepared to enable roller bearing axleboxes to be fitted to any existing bogies and it is hoped that any further new wheel sets will be so fitted. However, as several coaches have been equipped with new wheels fairly recently, not many more pairs are going to be required in the near future.

The first pair of bogies is being mounted on similar suspension arrangements to those adopted on the existing bogies, but the second pair, for No. 100, will have swing link suspension as on No. 14 (L. & B.). It will then be possible to compare the riding qualities of the two vehicles, from which a decision can be made for future editions. A point about the new coaches not previously mentioned is that their bogie centres are spaced so as to avoid wheels on both bogies passing over rail joints simultaneously—a fault with the existing stock where the bogie centres are about twenty-four feet apart.

Dealing with the new coaches in order of building, No. 24, the saloon coach which was pressed into service last August, has been in for finishing off details, particularly tables with modified legs. Externally, varnishing has been completed, a yellow band put above the windows of the first class compartment (we do not claim that to be an original idea) and a pair of thin red lines applied to the waist bead.

Progress continues on the new observation car, No. 100, and it is now virtually complete structurally, whilst "fitting out" proceeds steadily. This work is being done entirely by Fred Boughey and his volunteer carriage gang, who are always looking for more recruits to speed this very important work.

When space is available, work will start on No. 25. This is to be a standard saloon, first and third class, very similar to No. 24 but with the important addition of a lavatory compartment. It is planned that this vehicle will be in service before the end of the season.

After the routine autumn carriage overhaul programme had been completed, the three engines needing minor repairs were tackled. *Linda* had her driving wheels taken out for remetalling, a new smokebox hopper bottom was made and fitted and sundry other items attended to. *Merddin Emrys* had a pair of wheels removed for attention to a troublesome axlebox, which was found to be cracked—the seventh failure of this sort on the two Fairlies. Her water capacity was further increased by an extension to the tank not previously enlarged; she was fitted with a speedometer and also a steam brake, the one fitted to *Earl of Merioneth* in recent years. *Prince* also has been equipped with a speedometer and has had sundry boiler repairs, largely as a result of a false alarm due to longitudinal stays being bent. With three engines virtually ready for the start of the season—*Prince* was steamed for a heavy ballast working on February 6th—maximum attention can now be given to *Blanche*'s major overhaul as well as the new coaches and bogies.

Blanche was brought into the erecting shop on February 8th, and was very soon stripped right down to the frames, the boiler being lifted clear so that attention can be given to the cylinder fastening arrangements. These are one of the worst features of the design of these engines; the large cylinders are bolted to the smokebox side and supported by a weakly designed flange which forms part of the cylinder casting and is bolted to the frame. On *Blanche*, the R.H. flange is badly cracked and patched and the whole smokebox saddle is working in all directions. (*Linda*'s, too, is not solid, and will have to have similar treatment when she is next stripped.) A completely new fabricated saddle is being made which should make the whole engine more rigid.

Blanche's new tender is making good progress, and embodies several improvements as a result of experience. It is slightly longer than *Linda*'s, has straight sides and incorporates a tender cab; materials used are almost completely new. The water tank will be filled direct, not via the saddle tank, which will speed up refilling—an important matter in years to come when running beyond Tan-y-Bwlch begins. *Linda*'s tender is to be similarly equipped.

Permanent Way

The P.W. Department found good cause to be thankful for Minffordd goods shed during December, when some exceptionally wet weather made working in the open very uncomfortable. There are numerous jobs which can be done indoors now this large covered area is available, such as sawing sleepers, plugging the old holes and creosoting the raw ends. Having sleepers prepared in this way saves time at the relaying site, and it therefore follows that bad weather, in moderation, need no longer slow down the relaying programme. On the other hand, there are some unavoidable jobs that cannot be done under cover, and on two occasions flood squads had to turn out in torrential rain to clear culverts and ditches. Compared with other railways in the area the F.R. was let off lightly during the rains and floods of December 11-12th, perhaps thanks in part to the substantial amount of ditching done by volunteers in recent years. The only damage was just below Cemetery cutting; a blocked culvert at the top end turned the cutting into a fast-flowing canal. Some ballast was washed away, but after a couple of days' ballasting and tamping there were no ill-effects to be seen.

On Sundays December 13th and 20th the road crossings at Minffordd and below Penrhyn station were relaid. To eliminate joints within the crossing the two pairs of rails at Minffordd were welded together a few years ago; the same was done this time at Penrhyn with three pairs of rails, the total length being over fifty-two feet. With welded rails in selected chairs, packed with felt, screwed to ex London Transport Underground Jarrah sleepers, these crossings should stand up to anything that modern developments on road and rail may subject them to for many years to come, whilst experience has been gained for the relaying of the main road crossing at Penrhyn, which will have to be tackled within the next year or two.

Relaying is now complete from Cemetery through to Minffordd weigh-house, apart from the topping-up of ballast, and sections from Tro Keepers to Plas private station, from Whistling Curve to Tan-y-Bwlch bridge and at Tylers have been resleepered but, at time of writing, had not been ballasted and tamped. It is planned to use more than the normal amount of ballast between Three Gates crossing and Hafod-y-Llyn, in order to eradicate some variations in the gradient and lift the track in the wet cuttings; in some places the lift will exceed twelve inches. When this is completed it is important that any volunteers having cause to walk along this section (and, to a lesser extent, any ballasted section) should take great care not to disturb the ballast; not only to preserve the ganger's peace of mind but also to avoid constricting the ditches, which, if not flowing freely, will quickly magnify the work of a careless boot.

Sections of track scheduled for attention before Whitsun include Cei Mawr and the curve below, Penrhyn station down to Highgate and, at Easter, the bottom end of Minffordd station loop.

Engineering work done on neighbouring land this winter will have some effect on the Railway's scenery. Estates near Tan-y-Bwlch are being opened up by the Economic Forestry Group, who are building a road quite close to the line in the vicinity of Whistling Curve and Bryn Mawr. The same project has resulted in the felling of a birch coppice on the northern side of the line just before Tan-y-Bwlch bridge, opening up a new view for scenery-starved passengers on that side of the train. On a less satisfactory note, the National Grid power lines are being erected from Trawsfynydd to Anglesey and cross the line at Minffordd. An extra large pylon is being planted very close indeed to the top points; the Bron Turnor crossing had to be hurriedly relaid and lengthened early in February to take the heavy vehicles and machinery used in the erection of the pylon. Fortunately, the power lines are going underground across the Traeth so the priceless view from the Cob will not be spoilt, but pylons are being used across the Dwyryd Valley and can also be seen striding over the hillside from Penmorfa northwards.

Co-operation and Safety

We have referred before to the close behind-the-scenes co-operation existing between ourselves and the other "slim-gauge" lines. The Talyllyn Railway has good friends in Messrs. Smiths, through whom an ultrasonic flaw detector has been acquired at a favourable price. Nevertheless, such equipment is still quite costly to concerns such as ours, particularly in view of the very limited usage, and so the T.R. and F.R. have shared the cost equally, safe in the knowledge that the two concerns are not likely to need the equipment at the same time. So far it has not been used other than for trial and experimental purposes; correct interpretation of its indications will require quite a lot of experience.

Many of the older F.R. axles are of wrought iron which cannot be ultrasonically tested (their laminar nature makes them less susceptible to fatigue fracture anyway), but with more and more steel axles coming into use it will be necessary to carry out a regular programme of testing.

As the Railway grows and develops, so its mechanical organisation has to be improved and put on a sound basis. In the early days such things as carriage examination were done haphazardly when they could be fitted in, but nowadays they are done on a planned system. All carriage axles are now stamped with a number, and any changes are being recorded so that a life history of each one is being built up.

Matters such as this are constantly being added to the general administration of the Railway, but they all help to maintain the safety and efficiency which is the aim of all railway systems.

86.   Dduallt had slumbered peacefully since 1939, apart from the occasional slate or works train, but by the time that it was photographed in September there was much activity on the Deviation. The old no. 1 van body was in use as a store. (N.F.Gurley coll.)

87.   Another Army exercise was "Shish Kebab", when some regulars from Longmoor took over the FR to gain experience of operating an unfamiliar railway, as well as relaying a length of track. Houses now stand where the Army vehicles are parked. (N.F.Gurley)

NEWS FROM THE LINE - Summer 1965

Traffic

The start of the season is always a testing time for men and machines. The locomotives have been out of action for six months, during which time they may have been subjected to modifications and repairs. Coaches are inclined to be stiff and sluggish, in spite of intensive oiling and a trial trip or two. Rails are inevitably rusty and therefore very slippery when wet. Passenger traffic is a completely unknown quantity, varying greatly on weather conditions. It was probably a combination of these factors which made Easter Sunday this year an unhappy day for staff and passengers alike.

During the morning, *Prince* worked to Dduallt with a combined weed-killing and S. & T. train, then stood by at Tan-y-Bwlch, the idea being that she should return to Boston Lodge with the weedkilling equipment once the up passenger train had safely arrived, whilst the S. & T. train was to return by gravity much later. At Portmadoc, a seemingly never-ending stream of passengers turned up for the one (2-30) train. As the six-coach train had been overcrowded the previous day, an extra coach had been prepared, but even that was insufficient and a hasty decision was made to add four-wheelers 1 and 8 from the goods shed. Hurried cleaning and oiling enabled the train to get away at 2-45, which was very commendable in the circumstances. At Minffordd, *Linda* failed with a leaking tube, and had to be taken off the train; an SOS being phoned through to Tan-y-Bwlch for *Prince* and to Boston Lodge for *Moelwyn*. Shunting operations were hampered by the P.W. Dept's possession of the loop, which could not be used as such. Eventually, *Moelwyn*

returned to Portmadoc with one bogie and the four-wheelers with those passengers who had not time to continue the journey. Needless to say, it then began to rain, and *Prince* had great difficulty with the six-coach train on a very slippery rail, arrival back at Portmadoc finally being little short of two hours late. Later in the evening the S. & T. gang had a happy time pushing their train and the weedkiller down the grade—even gravity wasn't working properly that day!

Next day *Merddin Emrys* was steamed and yet another coach was prepared, but such are the vagaries of traffic that seven coaches were only comfortably filled. *Linda* worked again on the Tuesday, but traffic soon began to decrease and *Prince* handled most of the trains up to A.G.M. day when all three were actively employed. *Merddin* and *Prince* then shared most of the work up to Whitsun.

Traffic figures have so far shown a satisfactory increase over last year's. Although an increase at this time of year when traffic is comparatively light wouldn't, in itself, have much effect on the season's results, there is every reason to hope that the increase will be maintained with the help of Passenger Centenary publicity and we can report, as we go to press, a very busy Whitsun.

On May 24th the new Observation Car, No. 100, was launched with due ceremony and entered revenue-earning service next day, while No. 11 (the old "Obs") was shunted over to Boston Lodge to have inward-opening doors fitted so that the "B" train guard can use No. 11 rather than the kitchen

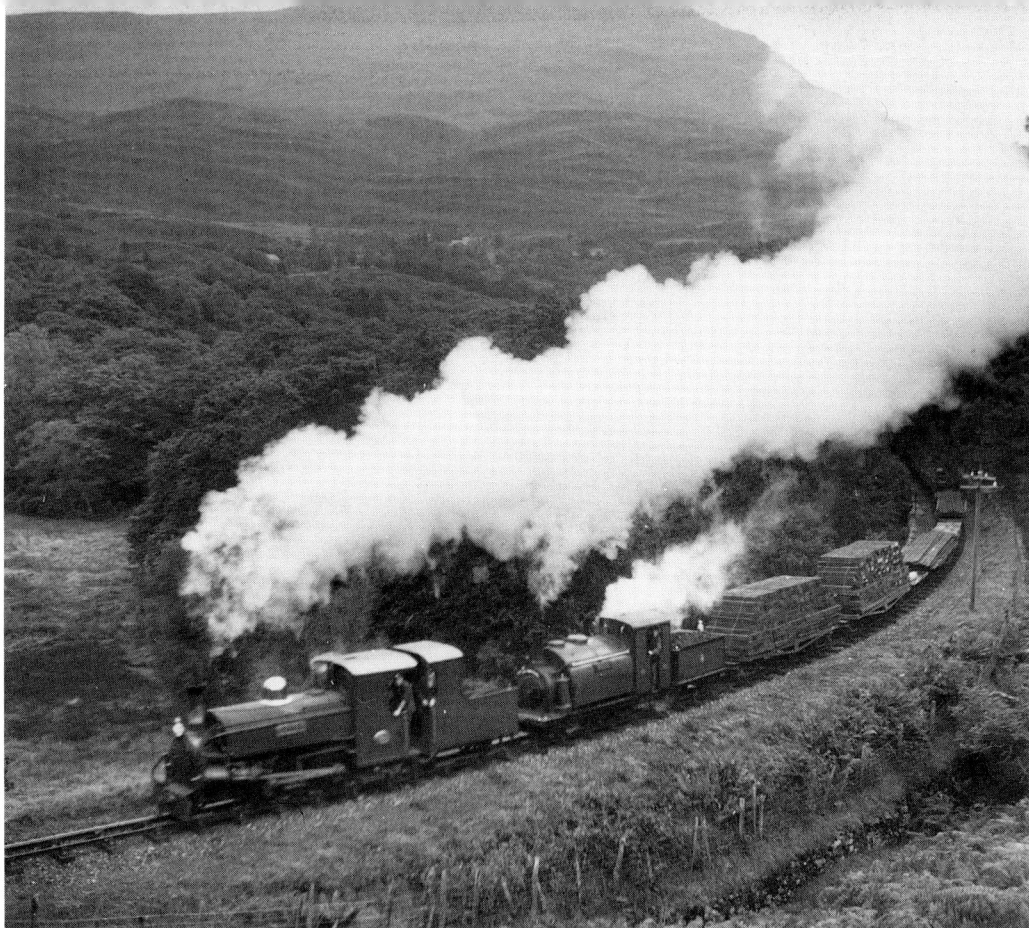

88. "Shish Kebab" involved some early starts (by FR standards); a massive PW materials train is seen on Whistling Curve at 08.00 on 17th September. *Blanche* is piloting *Prince* on the first day of the exercise. (A.G.W.Garraway)

portion of Buffet Car No. 12. (Last year van No. 12 for the same purpose.) The new "A" train minimum rake consists of Nos. 17 or 18 and 14 (Buffet) in green/ivory livery and 24 and 100 in varnished mahogany, the effect being quite pleasing. Interest is centred on the riding qualities of the two new vehicles in view of the different types of suspension employed (see Magazine 28, page 7). Both ride smoothly, but No. 100 with the swing link suspension seems very slightly to have the edge, perhaps due only to its superlatively luxurious finish throughout, which doesn't allow fair comparison with the third class portion of No. 24.

No. 100 richly deserves the attention it has received in the publicity world, and is proving a most popular attraction. Its observation compartment contains ten well-upholstered pedestal-mounted swivelling chairs. The usual compromise had to be struck between comfort and seating capacity, consequently typical Festiniog clearances prevail between the seats and they can only be fully swivelled with care. It is hoped that children will not try to spin on them, as this could have disastrous effects on their neighbours' knees. The other saloon is fitted with eight green ex-Pullman seats, with a table to each pair. Access to each saloon is through a vestibule equipped with a thick fibre mat, which should help to preserve the crested carpeting, the latter being fitted with underlay to enhance the luxury. The brake van portion has wide sliding doors and has been designed to hold two large prams or several bicycles. It is equipped with shelving for catering purposes and has a hand brake and vacuum setter although not intended for occupation by the guard in normal circumstances. Each partition has a sliding door; the corridor connection with No. 24 has been experimentally fitted with special rubber-edged gangways to improve the protection for anyone passing from one coach to the next. This feature is to be fitted to other end doors in due course.

Boston Lodge

Linda was retubed during late May and early June, re-entering service on Whit Sunday. *Blanche's* overhaul had to be suspended for a short while so as to give maximum effort to completing No. 100. Work has again been resumed in earnest and it is hoped that the engine will be in service for the peak season.

Some humourist(s) decided to contradict Mr. Wayne's assurances in Magazine No. 27, and *Palmerston* duly appeared in pink paint with *Harold*

Wilson on the nameplates for A.G.M. day. Perhaps it might have been more appropriate to paint such remains blue and name them *Ernest Marples*!

Works staff had a busy time preparing for A.G.M. day. The assembled wheels and axles for No. 24's new bogies arrived from Vulcan Foundry on the Friday afternoon. It took most of the evening to fit the wheels to the bogies and to mount the coach, then there was an early start next morning to connect and adjust the brake gear. The fact that the coach was able to run in the 11-00 train without delaying departure by more than ten minutes deserved a little more credit than some members seemed prepared to give.

A recent addition to the Railway's assets is parked on the standard-gauge siding at Minffordd. This is three-ton travelling manual crane No. 542, a standard Swindon production of 1937, weighing in all nineteen tons. Its main function will be to trans-ship heavy items from F.R. wagons to road vehicles or B.R. wagons and vice versa.

Permanent Way

The two Kango ballast tamping hammers have been very busy since early March and nearly all the recently relaid track has now been ballasted, set up and tamped. Supplies of good clean ballast are needed so that topping up can be completed.

For tamping, and also for drilling and chair screwing, the P.W. gang are no longer dependant on the old B.S.A. portable generator which has given spasmodically good service over a number of years. As the result of a very fine homework project in the London area they now have a rail mounted generator, driven by the Austin 7 engine which used to drive the shafting in Boston Lodge erecting shop. The machine actually entered service just after Christmas and has proved extremely useful on major work where total possession of the track is permissible. It is, in fact, only a stopgap, as a diesel generator is now being prepared for outdoor use while the Austin is earmarked for static duties in Minffordd goods shed.

With the exception of three or four isolated sections, which are now being tackled, it can be recorded that all the 15,000 or so sleepers between Portmadoc and Tan-y-Bwlch have been changed at least once since volunteers first started work on the Cob back in 1955. This is, of course, only a theoretical landmark.

NEWS FROM THE LINE - Autumn 1965

Traffic

"More passengers—but more headaches as well" sums up the traffic situation for this year, although as we go to press the headaches seem to have diminished whilst the figures continue to look very healthy.

The spring season was a short one, with only six weeks between Whitsun and the start of the summer service, compared with nine the previous year. Consequently, in spite of consistently good figures in June, no overall increase was recorded until well into July. However, after a couple of weeks of the peak season there was every prospect that last year's 144,000 was going to be exceeded, and 150,000 became the hoped-for target. The big query was how the changed date of August Bank Holiday would affect traffic, as we have nearly always had our peaks at the end of the month anyway. The result was three consistently good weeks, followed by a really remarkable week—commencing August 15th—when every record in the book was well and truly smashed; over 1,800 people travelled on the Tuesday, beating the previous best set up on August 5th, 1963, by more than 200, and the following two days were also above the old record. The week's passenger journey figure of 13,612 (excluding outside bookings) will take some beating. Perhaps it should be mentioned that the weather was just perfect from the Railway's point of view—dry, with quite a lot of sunshine, but always too cool for lazing around on the beach. The next week illustrated the effect that extremes of weather can have on traffic: Monday, Wednesday and Thursday, which were mainly dry but cool, brought daily booking figures in the region of 1,400, Tuesday was very wet and contributed only 900, whilst Friday, very hot and sunny, brought a miserly 630. Then came the Bank Holiday, with extremely good results over the weekend and on Tuesday, followed by a quiet Wednesday and Thursday but an inexplicably busy Friday. In the six weeks, July 25th to September 4th, over 72,500 passenger journeys were made (excluding outside bookings) once again showing the common transport problem of the "peak" periods.

Efforts have been made to boost the traffic figures with extra trains. On August 10th a trial run for Blanche leaving Portmadoc at 5.45 p.m. was advertised to the public and support was sufficient to justify running the train on Mondays to Thursdays throughout the rest of the summer season. This train fills a gap in the timetable and provides a convenient return service for late-afternoon passengers from Tan-y-Bwlch. Then on Sunday, August 15th, some passengers were somehow given the impression that they could make a return trip from Tan-y-Bwlch, and a special train had to be run from Portmadoc at 4.40 to get them back to their car. This train, too, though virtually unpublicised, was quite popular and was run on the three subsequent Sundays with excellent results. Some local traffic is also being attracted, for the first time for several years, thanks to the re-introduction of a cheap day excursion fare between Penrhyn (only) and Portmadoc, and some good publicity in the Upper Penrhyn area.

The season has not been an easy one from the operating point of view. Blanche did not enter service until August 17th, which meant that Prince had to be used very frequently until that date on trains which were much too heavy for comfort and in conditions which were sometimes rather difficult. Merddin Emrys had a bad spell early in August with valve rod and valve trouble on the bottom bogie, and ran paired with Prince on at least three days. Earlier in the season a crisis developed when forestry work high on the slopes of Moelwyn resulted in pollution of the Tan-y-Bwlch water supply and it was found that small locomotives do not function efficiently with quantities of peat in their pipes and boilers. About the same time some very slack coal made it hard going for the Festiniog thoroughbreds, though the Hunslets seem to thrive on it. Only when Blanche was back in service was it possible to get the locomotive roster back to last year's regular arrangement, and even then various events contrived to upset it. For instance, on August 24th the public water supply failed in the Portmadoc area and only Tan-y-Bwlch tank could be used. Merddin's tanks were empty and she could not be steamed, so Linda and Blanche had to work alternate trains, with Prince acting as pilot as required between Minffordd and Tan-y-Bwlch, for, ironically, it was a very wet day.

Train formations, too, have been rather unsettled; until Welsh Highland coach No. 26 re-entered service early in August a good deal of juggling was necessary between the two train sets to meet variations in traffic, and it was always important to keep Prince's load to a minimum. In spite of, or perhaps because of, the introduction of No. 100, first class accommodation has been as short as ever on busy days, but in general the balance between first and third class capacity has been very satisfactory. Both observation cars have paid their way handsomely; takings in 100's observation saloon have been 20% up on those of 11 last summer, whilst 11, running on the second train, has taken only slightly less than it did on the main train last year. Trade in the buffet cars has likewise been at a high level.

Popular additions to the facilities at Portmadoc and Tan-y-Bwlch have been good old pull-the-brass-handle platform ticket machines, ex-Chatham and Dorchester respectively. For 2d. they issue specially printed card tickets and, although there is no compulsion whatever for non-travelling visitors to buy them, something like fifty tickets have been sold from each machine daily, mostly to fare-paying passengers as souvenirs.

Boston Lodge

The main job for the summer has been the re-assembly of Blanche. Modifications have been along the same lines as those made to Linda, with reprofiling of the cab and provision of steam brake and vacuum gear for train brakes, though the sanding gear and other items still need attention. The present temporary matt black livery is due to be transformed into the standard F.R. green livery during the winter, but her very distinctive tender cab will make distant identification a simple matter.

At the same time, a good deal of labour was expended on rebuilding Welsh Highland open coach No. 26, the one retrieved from hen-house duties in 1958. It had been equipped with a new steel underframe last winter and has now had its bodywork rebuilt, with new panelling, strong seats bolted to the body framework to give greater rigidity and, most important of all, new full-length doors complete with glazed droplights. Upholstered seat cushions from scrapped buses have been provided, and as a result the coach is a much more comfortable vehicle, suitable for use in all weather conditions. It is in varnished mahogany livery, with the usual "3" transfers on every door, which, together with beading and the structural alterations, have changed its appearance completely. As its number has not yet been painted on, quite a few visiting enthusiasts have been puzzled by this "new" coach.

With the locomotives in service also requiring a good deal of attention, and unexpected work being necessary on one or two coaches, the works staff have been very fully occupied and work on the frame for new coach No. 25 has been put back until the autumn. During the annual working fortnight of the "Tadpoles" from Chace School, Enfield, the second road of Glan-y-Mor paint shop was lowered and a start made on concreting the floor area.

89. The half mile of track relaid by the Army was above Tan-y-bwlch. A special inspection train stands on the finished product on the approach to Garnedd Tunnel. The ledge on the right carried the original route of the FR until 1851. (A.G.W.Garraway)

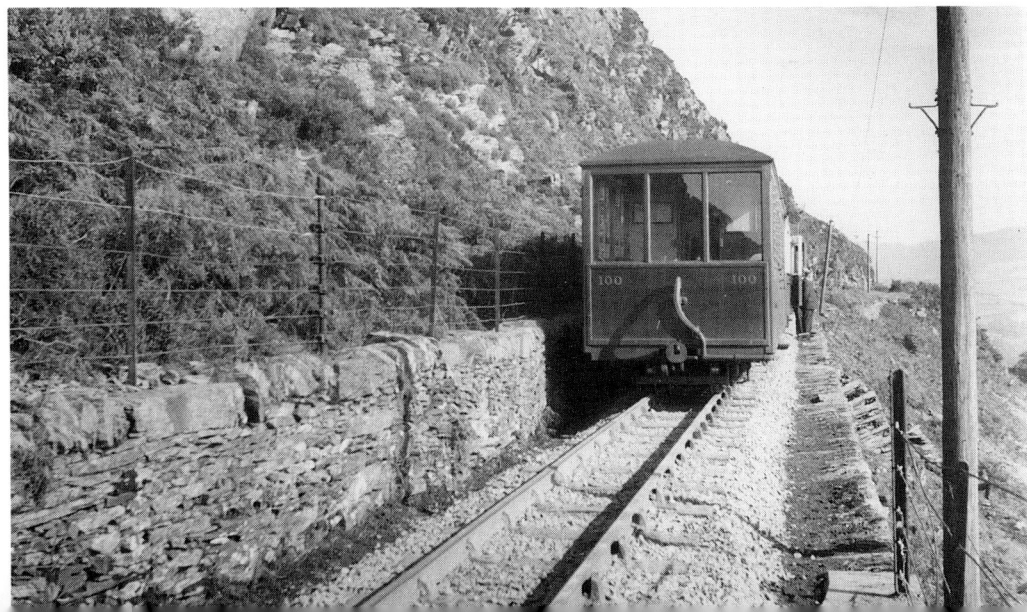

1966

NEWS FROM THE LINE - Winter 1966

Traffic

As we go to press, the season's passenger returns are just to hand. Journeys resulting from Portmadoc bookings, at over 137,000, are 8% up on last year. Through bookings from British Rail are well down, but, with those from coach tour operators slightly up, the final passenger journeys figure is 150,502. As this is coupled with a more-than-corresponding increase in revenue and a pronounced improvement in passenger comfort, there is good reason for satisfaction with the Passenger Centenary season.

September, which is normally a very quiet month after the first week or so, was enlivened this year by the arrival of army personnel to man the trains and stations, though F.R. staff and volunteers remained on hand to deal with the purely commercial side—ticket issuing and examining, sales, buffet car, etc. Passengers, though perhaps a little disquietened by the presence of so much khaki, had a good time of it; scheduled passenger trains were invariably made up to five or six coaches and usually hauled by *Merddin Emrys*. Many specials were put on at odd times, usually handled by *Linda*, and these proved beneficial to the inevitable would-be passengers who turn up expecting trains to be running every few minutes even at the end of the season. Another beneficiary was our good friend Jock, driver of the weekly Maidstone & District North Wales Tour, who always brings his passengers for a ride on the first up train on Tuesdays. The 11.00 a.m. off-peak departure is rather late for him and so a five-coach 10-30 special was put on for him two weeks running. As the Maidstone tourists only make the single journey, the special was held at Tan-y-Bwlch and combined with the booked train for the downward journey, a grand total of eleven bogie coaches hauled, or to be precise, braked, by *Merddin Emrys* and *Linda*.

The frequent materials trains run in connection with the relaying project at Tan-y-Bwlch and handled by *Prince* and *Blanche* rarely caused any delay to passenger traffic. On Thursday September 23rd, however, *Blanche* disgraced herself by becoming derailed near Gysgfa with the 9-00 a.m. ballast train which, on that occasion, consisted only of the engine and brake van. The army dealt with the situation very efficiently, but until mid-afternoon passenger trains had to terminate at Penrhyn. Next day a rare misunderstanding between control and the army driver of *Linda* resulted (after a very long story) in the 2.30 up passenger having to wait at Portmadoc until after 2.50, while Simplex shunted a Brigadier's special into Glan-y-Mor yard clear of the main line.

The troops left during the first week in October and the two Wednesdays Only trains then rounded off the season as far as paying passengers were concerned. However, after an enjoyable staff visit to Aberystwyth and the Vale of Rheidol line, there was still a week-end of great activity to come. After the hectic nature of the previous three months it was fitting that it should be a festive and happy week-end, with bright sunshine throughout; October 22-24th was the date.

Before and after working a ballast train on the Friday morning, *Prince* was subjected to a cleaning ritual rare, even on the F.R., for its thoroughness. It was the evening of the annual staff dinner and, as usual, a buffet car train was run to Tan-y-Bwlch and back to round up the staff and deliver them to Harbour Station. From there, Directors' and other officials' cars transported them to the Queens Hotel for an excellent informal dinner. Afterwards, the train, manned traditionally by volunteers, performed its earlier function in reverse, arriving back at Portmadoc well after midnight—with the liquor stocks in the buffet car well depleted, for by then it was the Manager's wedding day.

The wedding took place at St. Mary's Church, Tremadoc, and the reception was held at the Commercial Hotel, Portmadoc. Allan and Moyra then made their way to Harbour Station and, with the guests, boarded a special train, hauled by *Prince*, of course, on the first stage of their journey for their honeymoon in Scotland. No-one seriously expected the train to have a completely smooth passage—and it didn't. Lottie Edwards' crossing gates had somehow got locked with a non-standard padlock and there were mysterious patches of very dense and smelly fog (?) in places, contrasting with the colourful trimmings on Penrhyn crossing gates. Eventually the *Wedding Bell Special* arrived at Tan-y-Bwlch, where a car was waiting to take the couple to Blaenau Ffestiniog B.R. on the next stage of their journey, while *Prince*, still sporting white ribbons, took the guests, now augmented by volunteers from London and Hansag, back to Portmadoc.

Early Sunday morning, *Prince* was again steamed, and with Bill Hoole at the controls hauled a specially-prepared works train through to Dduallt, where a C.E.G. party were hard at work. The Directors and other officials present were able to witness a particularly large blast as well as inspect the workings and Dduallt mess, and some took the opportunity of helping to fill a skip with rock and spoil.

The remaining coaches were then put away for their winter's hibernation, and the Passenger Centenary season was over.

Boston Lodge

During the autumn, *Earl of Merioneth*'s boiler was prepared for hydraulic testing, and received the necessary approval on November 4th. Work will be proceeding with the completion of the overhaul and re-assembly during the winter; a good deal of work is still required, particularly on the bottom bogie. *Blanche* entered the paint shop early in October and after several week-ends of Don Hayter's expert care is now resplendent in F.R. green livery.

Welsh Highland coach No. 23 is at present in the erecting shop, undergoing treatment similar to No. 26. A new steel frame has been fabricated, bogies are being modified, and the coach has already been re-roofed as the first stage of the bodywork re-building. The frame has been built for new coach No. 25 and its bodywork will be arriving after Christmas. Meanwhile, bow-sider No. 17, the first of its type to be put back into service in 1956, has been undergoing extensive bodywork renewals in Portmadoc goods shed.

Permanent Way

Most of October was spent at Boston Lodge. The relaying and re-alignment of the carriage shed sidings was quite a major undertaking. The old layout may have been satisfactory when the shed housed locomotives, but the curves at the shed entrance were extremely hazardous for coaches. Clearances were sometimes a matter of millimetres rather than inches, and improperly opened doors have caused more than one mishap. The new layout gives much straighter entry into the shed, whilst the completely reconditioned pointwork will remove the element of suspense that has always accompanied shunting movements at this spot in recent years. The opportunity was taken of overhauling all pointwork in the area; the turnout from the main line at Pen Cob received particular attention, with renewed rodding and facing point lock.

As a result of good work by the army and volunteers soon afterwards, further improvements have been made to the layout at Glan-y-Mor. The old ash siding now fans out into three, the right-hand fork forming a new tip road whilst the other two sidings can be extended for a considerable length when labour is available.

Another useful job done, as a temporary measure, by the army was the interlocking of Minffordd bottom points, which are now operated by a ground frame conveniently situated on the down platform, pending the installation of the complete signalling system. This will greatly ease the stationmaster's job and help to speed up the crossing of trains at this station.

No time was lost in utilising the brand-new granite ballast left over from the army exercise, and several *Prince*-hauled ballast trains were run during the Hansag working fortnight in mid-October. November 1st saw the start of the winter track programme, with work being concentrated on setting-up and tamping several sections which have been awaiting this attention since re-sleepering. Week-end volunteer work has been mainly at Penrhyn, on the first stage of the relaying programme, which embraces the section from Pen-y-Bryn right through to the top end of the main road crossing above Penrhyn. As the track cannot be lifted appreciably within station limits, the main line and the ends of the loop are having to be completely dug out so that the old mixture of mud, rock and rubbish can be replaced by good ballast. The opportunity is being taken of extending the loop by some four rail-lengths—the maximum permitted by the location—and at the same time the top points and many other lengths of poor double-head rail are to be replaced with bull-head.

The situation above Tan-y-Bwlch is that the first 250 yards, relaid by volunteers in August, has not yet been ballasted and tamped; it is hoped that this can be completed next summer. From that point up to a few yards short of Garnedd tunnel, the track has been completely relaid by the army and, helped by about two-hundred tons of brand-new ballast, looks really magnificent—a credit to any B.R. track gang. It is only hoped that those people whose business takes them along the track on foot—including pushing trolleys—will treat it with the reverence it deserves, and take particular care not to trample down the ballast shoulders so carefully built up by the army platelayers. As far as the F.R. track staff are concerned, relaying of this section is a summer job, and no further work is programmed this winter.

The Deviation

Civil Engineering Group working parties have been going to Dduallt in steadily increasing numbers throughout the autumn. During September and October a hired compressor was on the site, and this enabled the gangs to break out the rock at the faces. Simultaneously, a programme of advance drilling was carried out, and over 100 holes, some of them 10 ft. deep, were sunk through the rock along the line of the future cutting. Appropriately on Guy Fawkes week-end these were charged with 130 lbs. of gelignite, and fired. The blasts resounded round the mountains for about five seconds, and loosened enough rock to keep all the available labour digging for three months.

Both cuttings are now roofed with tarpaulins on steel frames, which are moved forward as the work progresses, and have virtually eliminated delays due to wet weather. A pneumatic pump was tried in August in Site 3 cutting, which has tended to flood on account of the gradient, and this proved very effective. However, as blasting progressed, it opened fissures in the rock, and the cutting no longer floods.

On the site of Rhoslyn Bridge, the rock under the east abutment was found to be unsound. To stabilize it a number of holes were drilled down about 4 ft. to the secure rock beneath and 1½ inch steel bars grouted into these holes, thus reinforcing the rock prior to starting on the stonework.

It may be that some members of the Society can acquire some airline. This is an item of which we are particularly short, and any offers would be greatly welcomed by G. D. Fox, Project Engineer, Dduallt, Maentwrog, Blaenau Ffestiniog, Merioneth.

90. Part of the programme to improve track conditions was to eliminate joints in level crossings where it was impossible to maintain fishplates. Also, the PQR rail was only in 24ft lengths and so these were welded in pairs, on site, by the Thermit process. This is Penrhyn crossing in March. (A.G.W.Garraway)

92. A Kelbus sand drier was acquired from one of BR's redundant steam locomotive depots. Sand was loaded round the flue at the top. (J.F.Andrews)

91. First there was pre-heating of the rail ends and then ignition of the mixture of steel and magnesium in the crucible. This produced molten steel which ran into the joint, sealed by means of the moulds. After it cooled, the rail surface would be ground flush. (A.G.W.Garraway)

93. Few have seen the interior of a drier. As the sand became dry, it was able to fall through curved bars and it was removed through the small doors seen in the previous photograph. (J.F.Andrews)

NEWS FROM THE LINE - Spring 1966

Boston Lodge

During the winter all five active steam locomotives have received attention, and with more motive power due to arrive in the very near future it seems an appropriate time to summarise the locomotive situation.

Earl of Merioneth: The formidable task of fabricating new boiler cradles/ bogie centres was well in hand by the end of February, as was the overhaul of the bottom bogie and motion. Once these are completed, reassembly should proceed fairly rapidly, but it would be rash to forecast at exactly what stage of the operating season *Earl* will be able to take over heavy duties.

Merddin Emrys: The tubes have started to go and various firebox repairs are also required. As these would involve taking off the tanks and lagging, work is being concentrated on *Earl* which is in much better condition generally. *Merddin* will, however, be available for emergency and standby duties.

Linda: Attention is being given to the motion pins and various details showing evidence of the hard work she has done in the last two seasons.

Blanche: Apart from a few minor details, *Blanche* is now fully Festiniogized, with sanding gear similar to *Linda's* and, of course, green livery. Adjustments have been made to line up the tender with cab, but at the time of writing the flexible roof connection had not been fitted.

Prince: The driving crankpins have worn very peculiarly, and the wheels have gone to Vulcans for thorough checking and new crankpins. The axleboxes have been overhauled and remachined.

The Beyer-Garratt locomotive mentioned elsewhere in this issue arrived on March 23rd in three parts, being unloaded next day.

The three diesels are suffering various ills. *Moelwyn's* engine is getting badly worn, and general mechanical work is also long overdue. *Tyke* has proved an almost impossible engine to start, and, as it cannot be tow-started, has unavoidably been relegated to the back of the shed for long periods. However, an Ian Smart patent Mk. 1 starter—consisting of a petrol engine, gearbox and connection to the starting handle dog—will do the trick, once it itself has been started. *Simplex* broke a primary gearbox shaft recently, but a spare is available. It is doubtful whether any further spares can be obtained.

On the coaching side, the bodywork for No. 25 had not arrived by the end of February. Work was proceeding with the bodywork improvements to coaches 17 (bow-sider) and 23 (W.H.R.), the latter being varnished and awaiting transfers, whilst buffet car 12 has been re-roofed and fitted with linoleum flooring. Bow-sider No. 18 is also in line for bodywork attention once its sister has been returned to traffic. Midland Group's fourth rebuilt coal wagon, No. 21, is now in service, and some other wagon renewal work is in hand at Boston Lodge.

As always, the works staff have had to tackle a variety of miscellaneous jobs too numerous to detail, but one rather unpleasant duty in February and early March warrants mention. Contractors for the G.P.O. were laying a new P.O. cable duct along the Cob, mostly under the footpath side; it was agreed that the F.R.'s cables could be accommodated in the same duct and that the contractors would deal with the extensions to Harbour Station and Boston Lodge, in return for which the F.R. would assist with the movement of materials along the Cob. So it was that members of the works staff were taking it in turns to spend a day out on the Cob shunting suitable wagons back and forth with loads of pipes, ballast and spoil. Perhaps we should point out that the middle of the Cob on a winter's day is not the ideal location for a largely-inactive job, particularly in Festiniog semi-open cabs. *Tyke* really came into its own on this duty, as its narrow width would clear digging machinery and materials stacked close to the track.

Permanent Way

The pre-Christmas programme of ballasting, setting-up and tamping in several locations was duly completed, though only just, at least two members of the gang barely having time to organise the drying of their working clothes before setting off for home.

Early in January relaying started in the Penrhyn area, working upwards from Highgate Crossing (not Pen-y-Bryn as forecast in the last magazine, due to a reappraisal of priorities). Except for Penrhyn station bottom points and the fifty-foot length of welded rails leading from them over the crossing, all double-head rail was replaced with bull-head, mostly the Penrhyn Quarries Railway rail. Care was taken to match the rails as carefully as possible, following experience gained with the P.Q.R. rail above Tan-y-Bwlch; the sleepers used were some of the best ever handled on the F.R. and a substantial amount of new ballast was used. As a result, the track through Penrhyn should be by far the best on the line, and there will be some disappointment if this is not reflected in the riding quality. The top points presented a problem; they were being resited to lengthen the loop and it was obviously desirable to take the opportunity of relaying them in bull-head. Unfortunately, stocks of bull-head pointwork are very sparse and virtually nothing in that line has so far arrived from the P.Q.R. After much head-scratching a sortie was made to Blaenau Ffestiniog and it was found that the bull-head point at Glan-y-Pwll would fit nicely; this was duly dismantled and brought down on the Company's lorry, and is now *in situ* at Penrhyn.

Early in March the Penrhyn road crossing was relayed. This was a hard and complicated job, done in collaboration with the police and County Council, using a compressor for road-breaking equipment, selected sleepers and Thermit welded rail joints to give a continuous 120-ft. length. The rails used were from the P.Q.R. passing loop at Felin Hen, being in excellent condition with very little sign of wear. The bull-head/double-head check rail chairs were,

again, brought down from Glan-y-Pwll; the P.Q.R. don't seem to have gone in for check rails very much, our own stocks are very low and, cost apart, it was not possible to get new chairs cast and delivered in time.

Quite apart from the pointwork and crossings, the Penrhyn area relaying has presented many other complications. Well over 100-tons of mud, spoil and rubbish had to be removed from the vicinity by volunteers before the job could even be started, and the support received from, in particular, the London Area Group was well appreciated, not forgetting the Hansags who have provided parties on every date promised in spite of their distance from Portmadoc. Many volunteer man-hours were also spent removing vegetation, ranging from grass in ditches to several massive trees, the roots of which had been unsettling the retaining walls between Fron Goch and Mount Hazel (the scene depicted on the 1965 calendar now presents quite a different appearance). Three drainage culverts were laid in the vicinity of the bottom points, which have been prone to flood to an extent that ducks have been seen swimming between the rails on more than one occasion. Several bulging or non-existent walls have been rebuilt, and occupation crossings retimbered. At the station the old waiting room, used by the Co-op as a store until they moved to new premises in January, was cleaned out on a wet day and taken over as a permanent way store. The walls still exhibit typical "old F.R." reading matter— a 1929 F.R./W.H.R. timetable, conditions regarding the carriage of explosives and an exhortation to buy a farm in Canada, via the Portmadoc agent of the C.N.R.

The programme for March covers the relaying of two sets of points at Tan-y-Bwlch and the provision of a third to give access to a new siding, opposite the water tank, which volunteers will be extending during the summer. Some straightforward relaying is also scheduled at Bryn Mawr, and when the Post Office work is completed the Cob will need some attention as well.

The Permanent Way Department is now the proud possessor of a diesel-engined generator. The Lister engine, overhauled in a very praiseworthy volunteer "homework" manner, has taken the place of the Austin 7 engine to drive the generator for working the permanent way tools, and is proving more economical to run as well as being more reliable and easier to start in damp weather.

Thermit Welding on the F.R.

From time to time mention has been made in these columns of the welding of two or more lengths of rail to eliminate joints at inaccessible locations on boarded crossings, etc. This has always been done in the erecting shop, involving time-wasting transportation of the rails and limiting the length of the welded rail to about 60-ft.—the maximum which can be accommodated on the bolster wagons with safety. To enable welding to be done on the spot in future, the Company has invested in a complete set of Thermit welding equipment— a system extensively used on B.R.—together with sufficient specially-made moulds to weld fifty joints. A representative of the suppliers spent three days with members of the gang in mid-February, after which they were quite proficient and confident of their ability to get satisfactory results.

It is intended to weld not only joints which are inaccessible for maintenance, but also a number of those which, due to softness in the track bed, require much more than their fair share of maintenance. Some, for instance, on the fairly fast section of track at Rhiw Goch, need repacking several times each season, and in an intangible sort of way the welding of these would prove profitable in a very few years.

The system worked smoothly on Penrhyn road crossing, where eight pairs of rails were welded into one continuous length, close scrutiny being necessary to tell where the joints were prior to welding.

Deviation News

Digging has continued every weekend with steadily increasing parties; the total length of completed formation on Sites 2 and 3 had reached 580-ft. by the end of February. In January the deepest part of the swamp at Site 1 was blown up and the crater filled with rocks to prepare a foundation for the embankment. In addition drainage work has been carried out in the central field. At the mess a suitably manorial fireplace has been erected, incorporating a four-foot granite lintel which required six men to lift it, and employing a scaffolding system composed entirely of tinned fruit. The chimney is nearing completion.

Staff News

Once again there are no departures to report, but there is one very welcome addition to the staff, in the familiar form of Tom Davies. Tom first joined the F.R. way back in 1915 and was on the books until the closure in 1946; in fact he drove the last train of that era. On February 21st, 1966, he retired from full-time employment with Cookes Explosives Ltd. and rejoined the F.R. next day on a part-time basis. In the winter months he is being attached to the Permanent Way Department, working at present with Evie Roberts on walling and fencing. In the summer he will be back on his old job with the engines, sharing *Prince* with Bill Hoole.

We know all members will join with us in extending the warmest of welcomes to Tom, and hope that his second spell on the F.R. will be a long and happy one.

94. The Army successfully erected the Glan-y-Mor steelwork which had previously stood in Leeds. Cladding had to wait until the Summer of 1967, money being too short to purchase materials. The rolling stock continued to suffer from the weather. (J.F.Andrews)

95. The first two Beyer-Garratt locomotives were built in 1909 for a two-foot gauge railway in Tasmania. One was repatriated in 1947 by Beyer Peacock. When their works at Gorton were closing down, the FRS acquired this unique machine, although it was going to require a lot of doctoring as well as repairs if it was ever to work on the FR. Note the multi-gauge track required by an international locomotive builder. (A.G.W.Garraway)

96. The Garratt was split into its three basic components to travel to Portmadoc, coming on two lorries over the Crimea Pass on 23rd March. It remained on show at Harbour station for some time but never worked on the FR. It was later loaned to the National Railway Museum and work started in 1996 to restore it for use on the Welsh Highland Railway. (A.G.W.Garraway)

97. The FR used not only unusual motive power but also some road transport of historical interest. Trojan made motor cars at their works near Croydon from 1929 to 1932 and continued with light commercial vehicles into the 1950s. (N.F.Gurley coll.)

98. Viewed from Minffordd weigh-house roof, *Blanche* has much of the FR's historic rollable stock in tow on one of the Whitsun trains. The tiny "Bugboxes" were pressed into service at all peak times in the 1960s. (J.Ransom)

NEWS FROM THE LINE - Summer 1966

Traffic

The season got off to a bright start on 31st March, with a special train in connection with a polling day outing for a Bangor school. The first few days of the public service were notable only for the amount of shunting that was necessary at Tan-y-Bwlch while the new inspection pit was being finished off alongside the water tower. *Moelwyn* acted as station pilot until Easter Sunday, when the run-round loop became usable.

Easter can be relied upon to produce some interesting operating features. This year, eight coaches were needed on the Saturday 2.30, but the rail was dry and *Linda*, assisted by *Blanche* from Minffordd, went up in fine style. Sunday was enlivened by the variety of the traffic. *Wickham* opened the proceedings, running to Tan-y-Bwlch early on, followed by *Moelwyn* with a works train, some loaded ballast wagons being dropped off at Penrhyn. By the time they had been unloaded *Simplex* was waiting to leave Minffordd with an air compressor bound for Dduallt, and that had not long cleared Tan-y-Bwlch before the 2.30 passenger was on its way, with *Linda* and six packed coaches. *Blanche* followed with a 3.00 relief, but with heavy rain and a shortage of sand, was soon slipping badly and stalled at Gysgfa. *Linda* ran down light to assist without delay, and the inevitable late running was not excessive. Once both trains were back at Portmadoc an appreciative audience witnessed an involved shunt, which enabled *Linda* to get away promptly with 63, 12 and 11 on an S. & T. evening works special, passing a cavalcade—*Moelwyn*, *Simplex* and *Wickham*—at Minffordd. The last up train was a *Blanche*-hauled special passenger; the chartering party was conspicuous by its absence but twelve paying passengers and forty-five volunteers kept the buffet car staff fully occupied and ensured that the train paid its way. An enforced wait at Tan-y-Bwlch for clearance, coupled with heavy showers, hampered the S. & T. work, and their resultant 11.30 arrival back in Portmadoc was late even by S. & T. standards.

There seemed to be plenty of trippers in the area, and so two relief trains were run on the Monday, at 3.00 and 4.30, thus helping to set up new records for Easter week-end traffic. The last three weeks of April, however, will be remembered for the extremes of weather conditions rather than density of traffic, the snowstorms and bitter winds keeping holidaymakers by the comfort of their home fires. Nevertheless, the pre-Whitsun traffic figures showed a good increase over 1965.

A.G.M. day, 1966, will go on record as the sunniest ever; it was also the first time the special train from London has not been met by a double Fairlie at Minffordd. Any disappointment felt by visitors must surely have been dispelled by the impressive way in which *Linda* and *Blanche* handled their ten-coach train, probably the heaviest up train since the days of attaching slate empties to the rear. It was in fact the first time in this era that a properly arranged ten-coach train has been worked, as previous large trains have consisted of one train set being attached in front of the other. *Prince* followed with a relief train made up of the four-wheelers and observation car No. 11; this was *Prince*'s first passenger outing of the year. *Blanche*, immaculate in her new livery, was the star performer of the day, working the seven-coach morning train and the late-night Minffordd special as well as sharing the afternoon train. We are told her appearance was in sharp contrast with that of the "black 5" on the special from Banbury to Shrewsbury, although the two green class 4s which brought the train into Minffordd were quite well turned out.

Whitsun brought a lot of sunshine and a lot of passengers; in fact it was quite encouraging that the Railway was able to lure so many people away from the beaches in such perfect conditions. Almost every day broke traffic records of some sort or other, with the peak, as usual in mid week. Tuesday and Wednesday brought bookings figures in the 1100s, then Thursday, cooler and cloudy at first, recorded a fantastic 1,244. As the best Whit day from previous years was under 1,000, it is not surprising that the week's passenger journey figure of just over 11,500 showed an increase of more than 25% over Whit-week, 1965. This increase was only made possible by the introduction of the peak summer timetable for the week, with eight trains each way, Monday to Thursday; this kept the size of trains down to reasonable proportions, although every coach, including 22, was in use on the Thursday afternoon, when *Blanche*'s load on the 2.15 was seven bogies and six four-wheelers. *Blanche*, *Linda* and *Prince* handled all the traffic and, assisted by the dry weather, kept perfect time, the only late running being due to last-minute shunting to add coaches and stops to beat out lineside fires. A fall of rain at the end of the week was, for once, very welcome, although it was unfortunate that it coincided with the *Flying Scotsman*—hauled Gainsborough M.R.S. visit to North Wales. A seven-coach special was run, hauled by *Linda* and *Prince*, with three-course lunches being served en route to about forty of the passengers.

The traffic figures to date auger well for the season as a whole, although the thought of a 25% increase in an August week, with only the possible addition of one more coach, is sobering indeed. The traffic department will be watching progress on No. 25 with keen interest.

Boston Lodge

Work is proceeding as rapidly as possible on *Earl of Merioneth*, and by Whitsun the boiler had been lagged and both bogies were on their wheels. Provided no unforeseen snags arise she should be in service during August.

The bodywork for coach No. 25 arrived in time for assembly over Easter, and fitting out has continued most week-ends since. The toilet compartment embodying the most up-to-date product of Messrs. Elsan's experience in this field, is installed at the bottom end, seaward side, otherwise the coach is similar in layout to No. 24.

Permanent Way

Pointwork alterations at Tan-y-Bwlch were completed in April. The top point has been completely re-sleepered, and will be ballasted and tamped during the summer when the track above gets similar treatment. Immediately below, on the station house side, a new point has been installed and three lengths of a new siding laid; continuation among the trees is envisaged. Weighted levers now give catch-point protection to both platform roads, and the new siding is ideal for Dduallt-bound works trains and trolleys as well as P.W. Dept. relaying trains. At the bottom end of the station, the siding point has been moved down almost to the bottom point, with which it has been interlocked. This move has increased the car parking space, at the expense of the siding laid by volunteers two years ago; however, their labours were by no means in vain, as anyone who witnessed the Army manoeuvres last September will confirm—the siding saw more activity in a fortnight than it would otherwise have done in years. It was in fact the deterioration in the siding point towards the end of last season that necessitated its relaying and consequently the advancement of part of the longer term plan for the station.

Just before Easter a concrete-lined inspection pit was installed alongside and just above Tan-y-Bwlch water tower. P.W. volunteers dug the hole, and the Mechanical Dept. were responsible for the concreting.

The Wednesdays-only train service in May gives the P.W. Dept. track occupation for several days at a time, and this year the opportunity was taken of laying in more Thermit-welded rail—two lengths each of 120 ft., at Rhiw Goch. The rails were welded into 60 ft. lengths at Minffordd before being transported to the site, and as this method proved satisfactory there is a long-term plan for a covered welding bay at Minffordd to enable this work to be done in damp weather. (This is not only for the comfort of personnel. Thermit welding cannot be done in the rain unless protection is provided, and the F.R. has not yet invested in the "umbrella" equipment produced for the purpose.)

Deviation News

Civil Engineering Group working parties have been to Dduallt on every week-end during the last quarter, and on all but two occasions digging was taking place on both Sites 2 and 3 simultaneously. As the number working has improved, more emphasis has been placed on output, which is now about twice what it was last autumn, up to 40 truckloads being dug on a good week-end. Over Easter, 125 loads were shifted (1 truckload = 1 cubic yard loose = 1¼ tons).

On Site 1, further bog blasting has been carried out, clearing the swamp from the embankment base for about 50 feet. Temporary track has been laid near the embankment base to complete the "borrowing" of the existing bank.

Formation length on 22/5/66 was 700 feet. "Ffestergraph" (cumulative output) for 1966—607 loads.

The Mess is complete, and often full at week-ends. A new path to it was blasted at Easter and should be finished during the summer. Plans for a siding at the Mess, to match that at Tan-y-Bwlch, have been approved, and work is about to start on levelling the ground for it.

The main effort for the next quarter will continue to be applied to driving the cutting between Sites 2 and 3, where about 100 feet remains to be dug. It is proposed to start a major borrowing site along the side of the station, to supply the 3,500 loads needed to complete Site 1, and, in doing so, to enlarge the station area.

99. The chutes had received concrete supports in 1964, the year in which the goods shed at Minffordd, and the attached iron shed, were vacated by a sawmill firm. The PW Dept. then took over the premises. *Moelwyn* is about to leave with ballast in ex-RAF Hudson wagons on 2nd July. (S.Evans)

100. The FR manages from time to time to secure contracts for location shots for films, bringing in useful additional revenue, though not without much extra work. Local ladies were recruited as extras for "Hand me my sword, Humphrey" and posed at Minffordd on 22nd July. (A.G.W.Garraway)

NEWS FROM THE LINE - Autumn 1966

Traffic

As a remarkable season draws to a close, the big question is not "How many?" as much as "Why?" Was it the seamen's strike causing people to cancel their continental holidays that brought so many to North Wales, or were there less obvious reasons for the glut that brought extra prosperity not only to the Festiniog but to the Talyllyn and other concerns as well? Next year may provide the answer, but in the meantime we can justifiably gloat not only over this year's figures, but over the way in which they were earned as well.

The most satisfactory aspect of the season has been the consistent increase in passenger figures during June and July (and, if present trends continue, September)—the months when we could carry twice as many without being extended. Each week from mid-June until the end of July recorded an increase in the region of 1,000 passenger journeys over the same week in 1965, representing gains of about 20-25%, and the first week of the autumn service did even better. During August, too, weekly gains were recorded, but not in the same proportions; nevertheless, the total number of passenger journeys for 1965 had been passed by August 31st, leaving the whole of September to supply our season's increase. Although the traffic in that month last year received a boost from the Army operations, we can still confidently expect another 25,000 journeys, to give a final total well up in the 170,000s.

Looking at the figures for individual days, the old record was soundly thrashed as early as August 4th, with 1,737 bookings. Then came a staggering 1,863 on August 17th (a cloudy Wednesday after a very hot Monday and Tuesday) followed by 1,651 on the Thursday. The most satisfactory week of all was that ending August 27th, with a record 14,476 journeys, for thanks to the cloudy weather the traffic was evenly distributed throughout and there were no uncomfortably busy days—not even a 1,500 was recorded.

Until August 30th all trains were handled by Linda, Blanche and Prince, with only Merddin Emrys, very dead at the back of the shed, in reserve, yet the timekeeping was of the highest order and it is difficult to recall a late arrival, during August at any rate, which could fairly be booked against the locomotive. With the smaller engines coping so well, it was felt unwise to steam Merddin unless absolutely necessary, as she was of most value as a usable reserve engine, but with the end of the peak season in sight and the prospect of the new coach entering service, she was steamed on Monday, August 29th, and worked trains on the following three days and also during the following week.

It had been obvious by early August that the new coach would not be helping to take the brunt of the peak season traffic, and so other means had to be devised to spread the load of the increased traffic. The result was an extra morning train, leaving Portmadoc at 10.10 and Tan-y-Bwlch at 11.20 on arrival of the 10.40 up. Butlins were very happy to take their passengers by coach to Tan-y-Bwlch for the single journey on the 11.20 down instead of the 10.40 up, and thus the new train helped to relieve the 10.40, which had been much too busy for comfort on many occasions. The 10.10 was intended as a morning trip for Prince, but on one occasion, when there were well over 100 ordinary passengers and Butlins promised another 112, Blanche had to be hurriedly summoned to take over the seven-coach train at Pen Cob and Prince went back to work the 10.40 instead. Prior to the introduction of the 10.10, Prince had been rostered for the 1.10, but this, too, had been made up to seven bogies more often than not, on which days the only trains light enough for Prince had been the two evening trips. An extra train was also run on Sundays, 12.00 noon from Portmadoc and 1.00 from Tan-y-Bwlch, and this was quite well patronised.

An interesting change this year was the switching of the train sets, mainly with the idea of reducing the amount of shunting necessary at Portmadoc. This permitted the "A" set to work the two evening trains and to complete five return trips, Monday to Thursday, against the "B" set's three or four. Last year a shunt was necessary at 7.10 p.m. to put the "B" set into the siding and the "A" set into the platform, which left little time for Prince to be prepared for the 7.30.

At the end of last season, when the 5.45 was introduced experimentally, a roster was devised using three train sets. This system has been continued this year, with a guard and two or three buffet attendants in each crew. The roster ensured that no crew had to work a twelve-hour day without adequate breaks and gave each crew at least one "free" day in the week, this usually being spent on minor repairs to coaches or assisting whichever department happened to be short-staffed.

The season has not been without its exciting moments. One such was on June 9th when Linda broke a spring hanger on the 3.35 down. To enable a relief engine to reach the train she was shunted into Penrhyn loop, but became derailed when setting forward over the bottom points. The 4.30 up had to be cancelled, and half-a-dozen passengers with return tickets were surprised to find themselves returning to Tan-y-Bwlch on a special train for the Blaenau Ffestiniog Musical Society (Allan Garraway was Producer of "The Mikado" last March) and enjoyed the three-course dinner which was served en route. On August 4th, towards the end of a very busy day, a coach was derailed at Portmadoc and the 5.45 arrived somewhat late, with the observation and buffet cars in reverse order, the train having been marshalled over the west-end points where there is only room for one engine and coach in the headshunt.

The firebar crisis, explained under the Boston Lodge heading, caused some anxious moments in operating circles. The worst occasion was when Linda shed four bars after the 12.56 down had been delayed thirty minutes waiting for a pre-booked party whose coach had broken down quite close to Tan-y-Bwlch. Equipping an engine in steam with new firebars is not the pleasantest of lunch-time occupations for engine crews, but with the inevitable accompaniment of bad language and burnt hands four new firebars were fitted and the fire relit, using a pile of logs. Prince took the 2.15 (six bogies and the bug boxes) to Minffordd, with a somewhat unhelpful Linda from Pen Cob. By that time the fire had recovered and the passengers arrived at Tan-y-Bwlch only five minutes late (and that due in any case to the earlier late running) blissfully unaware of the struggles which had taken place.

In spite of the absence of any additional coaches there has again been an improvement in passenger comfort, thanks mainly to the efforts of the passengers themselves. Off-peak trains such as the 1.10 have received better support, with a consequent lessening of "sardining" on the 2.15 except on the busiest days, whilst there has been a really substantial increase in first-class patronage during June and July. (There is little scope for an increase in first-class bookings during August, as demand has exceeded supply on peak-hour trains for some years.) On June 21st a new record was established when 68 first-class tickets were sold for the 2.20 and the nine-coach train included every coach with first-class seats except the second observation car. Linda coped unassisted, by the way. Thereafter a relief was run on busy days, and it seems probable that next year's timetable will see the 3.00 train running throughout, which means that mammoth 2.20s will be largely a thing of the past.

1967

NEWS FROM THE LINE - Winter 1967

Traffic

Any fears that September might prove an anticlimax to the 1966 operating season were soon dispelled; the remarkable and consistent increase in off-peak traffic was sustained right up to the last day of the season, when a cheerful party of members of the Multiple Sclerosis Society helped to boost the day's figures. With figures still required from one or two coach operators, the final total for the season is expected to be very close to 174,000 passenger journeys— a very satisfying figure and by far the most pronounced increase since 1960.

The increased figures from bookings on the Railway have not been matched by the inclusive tours, and many show a slight decrease over 1965. Whilst, on the surface, this may seem a little disappointing, it does not give any cause for concern as far as the financial aspect of operating the Railway is concerned. The timing of many of the tours necessitates use of the busiest trains, always for a single journey only, and often with no likelihood of a balancing coach party for the return working. The concessionary fares offered to attract tour operators are below the ordinary fares, whilst the reservation of compartments takes labour and time, and sometimes causes inconvenience to other passengers. It is generally felt that the present level of tour passengers is satisfactory, and if traffic can be increased, or even maintained, without an increase in tour traffic, it will be all to the good.

On the Saturday morning the Society was host to the Association of Railway Preservation Societies. *Blanche* hauled a train of the four "standard" coaches to Garnedd West, where the representatives of most of the active preservation societies were able to enjoy one of the finest views obtainable from a British railway carriage window while eating an excellent luncheon. While the A.R.P.S. tri-annual meeting was taking place at a Portmadoc hotel during the afternoon, the 2.30 was proving quite a busy train. A diesel railcar excursion was bringing an extra hundred passengers from South Wales, and this boosted the train to eight coaches—a worthwhile last outing for *Merddin*. Elsewhere in Wales, the T.R.P.S. special was arriving at Towyn and another enthusiasts' special was bringing blue 100 m.p.h. stock into Blaenau Ffestiniog; the first week-end of the autumn was a colourful one on the Welsh railways.

1967 Timetable

In view of the early start to the season, it is hoped that the 1967 timetable leaflets will be ready in time for insertion with this Magazine, but in case that does not prove possible we are detailing the early season arrangements. The service will commence on 24th March and operate daily until 20th April, then Wednesdays only until just before Whitsun. Departures will be at 11.00 and 2.30 from Portmadoc, and 12.00 and 3.35 from Tan-y-Bwlch, but the morning train will not run on Saturdays and Sundays. Extra trains will run at Easter if required, but as it falls so early demands are not expected to be heavy.

When compiling the timetable, great difficulty was found in assessing the probable Whitsun traffic, as this is the first year of the new arrangement by which a new Spring holiday is created at the end of May and Whit Monday (15th May) is no longer a Bank Holiday. There seems to be no unanimity amongst Education Authorities; senior guard Alan Heywood—an ever-present at Whitsun—was horrified to discover that his school was scheduled to return to work on the new Bank Holiday. A telephone call to his headmaster had the position rectified, but it remains to be seen how many other families will find themselves with parents and children on holiday at different times—and how that will affect our traffic.

Boston Lodge

The reassembly of *Earl of Merioneth* went very smoothly, considering the very thorough nature of her overhaul; by the end of November the outstanding work concerned auxiliary equipment such as speedometer, sandpots, draincocks and ashpans. Steam testing will not take place until the spring, when of course the engine will have to be run-in on suitable light loads.

Blanche has been in shops for routine attention to various fittings, motion and smokebox door. *Linda's* driving wheels have been removed for new crank-pins to be fitted, and a number of sundry maintenance jobs remain to be done. Both have been prepared for the boiler inspector's annual visit.

Prince is shortly to be partially dismantled to enable the smokebox to be lifted clear of the framing so that attention can be given to leaks in the bottom of the front tube-plate area; other routine work on this engine is held up pending rectification of this trouble and completion of the other three locos.

Moelwyn has been in the erecting shop since August undergoing the first phase of its long-overdue overhaul. A new (well, secondhand) Gardner 4LK diesel engine has been fitted and faults in the directional gearbox rectified. A new cab side now matches that on the driver's side, and a lot of auxiliary equipment has been overhauled and repaired, including dynamo, radiator, batteries, brakes and bonnet. The loco will be returning to service shortly, but will need to be taken into shops again at a later convenient date for replacement of driving wheel axle-boxes and rod brasses.

The Simplex, *Mary Ann*, has been deputising for *Moelwyn* on shunting duties, including some arduous P.W. trains to the section above Garnedd. Its 4LK engine was obtained as scrap, and when it gets hot the oil pressure at tickover is negligible. Since the advent of *Moelwyn* it has had little attention and often stands idle for long periods, but when *Moelwyn* is not available Simplex rarely fails to come to the rescue.

In anticipation of very heavy duty as relaying approaches Dduallt, the Wickham trolley has been given a general overhaul, including the fitting of a reconditioned engine and a new driving axle.

Three underframes for new coaches are at present under construction together. Although only one is required immediately, the first to be finished can be used as a full-size jig for the fabrication of the other two with, it is hoped, a marked saving of time on squaring and marking off. The latter two will only be welded strongly enough for transporting, and can then be returned to shops for completion at some date nearer the time they are actually required by the body builders.

Bow-sider No. 18 is currently receiving the same treatment to its bodywork as No. 17 had last winter, but as the ventilator hoods all came off without damage it will be possible to refit these and thereby reduce the bare appearance. The best doors from 17 and 18 are being used on 18.

An oxy-acetylene profile cutting machine has been installed and should prove a boon in the mass production of parts for general plate work, etc. An additional lathe is expected shortly and will help to relieve the shortage of turning capacity often felt at present.

Permanent Way

Work has been concentrated on relaying towards Dduallt throughout the autumn, and by Christmas the track-work between Tan-y-Bwlch and Coed-y-Bleiddiau should have been virtually completed, except for the nineteen lengths through Garnedd tunnel and a tremendous amount of walling and fencing. The 100-plus rail lengths from Garnedd to Coed-y-Bleiddiau have been relaid in approximately four months, although the P.W. gang has been depleted, due to holidays, for some of that period and volunteer effort has not reached unprecedented heights. Just over 200 lengths to Dduallt remain untouched, but the track bed is in worse condition than the section already dealt with; there are several very wet cuttings, the worst of which will have to be drained before any further relaying can be done. In the hope that good numbers of volunteers will be present at Easter, A.G.M. and other spring week-ends, to assist with drainage and turfing as well as loading and unloading materials trains, relaying of this section is being suspended during the early months of 1967, when the focus will be on the bottom end of the line. Harbour Station platform road is to be relaid, with particular emphasis on the inspection pit, and all the pointwork will be overhauled. The main line points will be moved further out on to the Cob, near to their original position, to give space for an additional turnout, from which a siding will be laid in 1968 nearer to the sea wall to accommodate the extra stock and third train set. A small head-shunt will be provided, like the one at Pen Cob, to enable light engines to enter the sidings from the station loops without fouling the main line. It is hoped that time will also permit some relaying to be undertaken on the Cob itself, at least as far as the signal. Dismantling of the platform road was begun by volunteers on December 10th-11th and large amounts of ash and oil-cake ballast removed.

To avoid mixing double-head and bull-head rail, only Penrhyn Quarry Railway bull-head rail is being used between Tan-y-Bwlch and Dduallt. However, some of the double-head rail thus released is about the least worn of any on the Railway and is being earmarked for use on the lower sections. Other lengths, particularly on the curves, are too worn to serve any useful purpose on the main line, and are being cut up, either into 5 ft. lengths for scrap or into 12 ft. lengths for use as temporary way on the deviation.

Deviation News

The Civil Engineering Groups have dug regularly every week-end of the last quarter. London "A" Group regained the Golden Spade by blasting and shifting 77 cu. yds. on 7th-8th October. The Ffestergraph stands at 1590, and the track length at 990 ft. on 20th November.

In the main cutting, Sites 2 and 3, all the rock between the faces has been blasted, and only remains to be dug out. Junctioning should occur early in January, when the Groups are running a digging fortnight. On Site 1, a three-way point has been installed to enable three skips to be loaded in the quarry simultaneously, which will be very necessary when this becomes the main working site in 1967.

A tramway has now been laid across the field from the station to the site of Rhoslyn bridge, and a special lightweight trolley built to work up the steep gradient. This is being used to carry material to the bridge site, and already about half the stone has been stacked there.

In view of the need to accelerate the work, plans are now under consideration for a massive expansion of the Groups. Details of this should be fixed before publication of the next Magazine.

Staff News

Everyone will be very sorry to hear that the General Manager has been badly indisposed since the latter part of September, and for nearly two months has hardly been out of doors. He is now slowly getting better and it is hoped that a visit to a warmer climate in December will have completed the cure.

The first change in the Railway's permanent roll-call for well over a year took place early in October, when Anthony Massau left the Railway after working with the P.W. Dept. for two years. A permanent replacement arrived during November, in the form of Paul Anderson, an active London Area Group member for several years. Paul has been a fireman at Nine Elms depot of late, and as a sideline has spent much time cleaning Bulleid Pacifics for enthusiasts' tours out of Waterloo. Another Londoner, Malcolm Vincent, who has had some P.W. experience on L.T.'s Northern line, was also working with the gang in November. The P.W. Dept. was further reinforced when Tony Massau returned for another spell of platelaying, as his Government training course had been unexpectedly postponed for several months.

101. Dduallt was to become the terminus for trains in 1968 so a run-round loop would be needed; to get space for a platform and a loop, considerable excavation was required. The spoil from this created the first part of the new line, here seen on the left going out to meet the embankment being built from the spoil from a cutting east of Dduallt station. (A.G.W.Garraway)

NEWS FROM THE LINE - Spring 1967

Traffic

The locomotive mileages for 1966 were as follows:

Locomotive	1966 Season	Total under Present Administration
Prince	.. 4,095	34,946
Merddin Emrys ..	.. 206	11,924
Earl of Merioneth ..	.. —	21,145
Linda	.. 4,824	14,986
Blanche	.. 2,783	5,385
Moelwyn	.. 803	16,446
Simplex Tractor ..	.. 359	1,502
Wickham Trolley ..	.. 2,353	4,757
Tyke	.. 120	180

Perhaps at this time of year some details of the coach mileages will be digestible. The total number of coach miles increased from 56,331 in 1965 to 62,338, an increase which, it will be noted, was not as pronounced as the growth of traffic. Buffet Car No. 14 ran a record for any coach of 7,201 miles, with Nos. 24 and 100 only a few behind. An interesting point is that ex-Welsh Highland coaches Nos. 23 and 26 ran 2,913 and 3,311 miles respectively; as neither has exceeded 2,000 miles in a season before, the usefulness of their conversion to closed coaches with upholstered seating is amply demonstrated. At the other end of the scale, the bug-boxes covered 1,037 miles each, which was, regrettably, no fewer than usual. "Banana boat" No. 22, which was only used when absolutely necessary, showed a decrease from 2,453 in 1964 and 1,777 in 1965 to 827 in 1966. When this vehicle has been rebuilt with steel frame and comfortable upholstery it will be equivalent to a Welsh Highland as far as the mileage figures are concerned.

The total number of train miles run was 10,090, making the *average* length of train equivalent to just under six bogie coaches.

Looking ahead to the 1967 season, it may have been noted that the time-table has a more rationalised look than for some seasons past; a train leaves Portmadoc at 2.30 on every operating day and such variations as there are in the day-to-day timings of specific trains have been kept to a minimum. The peak season bus from Tan-y-Bwlch to Blaenau, which was not very well patronised last year when it connected with the 2.15 from Portmadoc, will this year leave Tan-y-Bwlch at 12.50, as in the Spring service. There are no completely non-stop runs, but in the peak service there are no less than five 35-minute runs with one or two request stops—indicative, perhaps, of the plans for the Dduallt service in 1968.

The General Manager's volunteers wall chart is beginning to look reasonably healthy in the August column, but there is plenty of space still to be filled. He would particularly like to have some new names to chalk up, and preferably in May, June, July and September. The situation may change, of course, but there are completely blank spaces in the general traffic duties section for the weeks commencing 4th, 11th and 25th June, and from 10th September onwards.

Boston Lodge

With four weeks to go to the start of the season, *Linda* awaits the return of her driving wheels which have had new crank-pins fitted. A complete new set of rod brasses has been machined, whilst other parts that still require attention include the smokebox door, front mud-doors and engine/tender drawbar.

When *Linda* vacates the wheel-drop, *Earl of Merioneth* can receive some attention to foundation ring corners, have ashpans fitted and be weighed for final spring hanger adjustments, then the Fairlie will be ready for steam testing. A start has been made on painting her tanks and cab.

Blanche was steamed for valve adjustments on 1st March and the following day worked a heavy P.W. train from Minffordd to Coed-y-Bleiddiau. On 3rd March she powered the first passenger train of the season: a four-coach special for a school party.

Prince has been partially stripped down and the boiler raised clear of the frames to give access to the bottom front tube plate area.

Moelwyn has been back in service for some weeks, looking much more like a Festiniog engine should, with gloss finish and transfers. She sounds impressive, thanks to twin exhaust pipes which enable her to give a passable imitation of the Sulzer machines now used on the Cambrian freights. She now has a full cab backsheet and heater, and as time permits the whole cab will eventually be enclosed, making her drivers' lives more tolerable when shunting duties in winter drag them away from the warmth of the erecting shop. Work is in progress on the construction of rear sandboxes (she runs facing downhill) and the fitting of a hydraulic system for driving auxiliaries such as radiator fan and large ejector.

Simplex *Mary Ann* now performs nearly all P.W. shunting duties with drivers from that department—a mutually beneficial arrangement.

The first of the three new carriage underframes now under construction is at the fitting-out stage and nearly all the framework and sub-assemblies of the other two are ready for putting together.

The coaching stock is undergoing its annual winter checkover of running gear. No. 17 in particular has required much work on both bogies, with the wheel flanges being built up by welding and axleboxes linered and refitted into horns that have had to be completely re-squared and plated up; much of the brake rigging has been renewed, using new standard components, and the bolster suspension units have also been modified to the latest improved design.

Buffet Car No. 14 is being stained and varnished after thorough rubbing down; this means that the basic main train set will be in varnished livery this summer and the basic "B" train in green and ivory.

The rebuild of No. 18 is now complete. The re-use of ventilator hoods and of selected doors from 17 and 18 has helped to preserve more of the traditional appearance of the bow-siders than was the case with No. 17. The yellow strip above the first-class compartment—a standard feature of the varnished livery—would have been broken by the ventilator hoods, and so the vertical panels on either side of the first-class compartment have been painted yellow instead. (This should effectively dispose of the numerous "Metroland" jokes heard in the vicinity of 17 last A.G.M. day.)

Progress is being hastened with the rebuilding of the last large bogie coach to be tackled—No. 16—and the re-roofing with double-thickness plywood is almost complete. All the body work on this coach has been done by volunteers, and it is felt appropriate that the mechanical work should be similarly done; a "contract" has in fact been let with a volunteer group.

An appreciable amount of work has been undertaken for the P.W. Dept. lately. The largest job has been the re-conditioning of the old works pillar drill and the electric motoring of same. This will be installed in Minffordd goods shed to permit chairs, etc. to be drilled independently of the works. Three point crossing noses have been repaired, built up and hard-faced by welding in connection with the track work at Portmadoc.

The wheel lathe, often used for the Talyllyn 2 ft. 3 in. gauge as well as the F.R.'s 1 ft. 11½ in., has now seen service for the 15 in. as well, wheels from the Fairbourne Railway having been turned during February. It is claimed that Boston Lodge could cope with any wheels from "O" gauge to standard!

The new lathe has at last arrived and is in the process of being installed in the machine shop. Part of the blacksmiths' shop has been made over to the S. & T. Dept. as a pointfitters' workshop and store.

Volunteers Required: The Mechanical Dept. is always pleased to welcome persons skilled in its various trades. In addition, volunteers with experience in glazing and bricklaying would gladly be found work in the pattern loft, foundry and blacksmiths' shop areas, where much glass needs replacing and redundant doors and windows require bricking up.

Permanent Way

The complete programme of alterations at Portmadoc, outlined in the last Magazine, was modified in view of the heavy commitments further up the line and the non-availability of certain pointwork components. The compromise plan covered the all-important relaying of the platform road and a small portion of the main line on the Cob, but left, for the time being, the provision of turnouts for additional sidings and alterations to the existing loops.

The inspection pit in the station has been tackled in two ways. At the bottom end, just over three rail-lengths were relaid with ordinary cross sleepers and the intermediate spaces were filled in with more, poorer quality sleepers; thus the pit at that end is completely roofed over, except for two metal inspection covers, and no litter and earth can get in and block the drain at the bottom end. The surface is a vast improvement on the old continuous string of metal sheets held precariously in position by rotting timbers, and should be appreciated by staff and volunteers servicing trains standing in the loops when the platform road is empty. At the top end, where the pit is regularly used for carriage inspection and less regularly for running repairs to locomotives and stock, longitudinal sleepers are being used, rag-bolted into the brickwork below. Both cross and longitudinal sleepers bed on a three-inch layer of new concreting on top of the existing brickwork; the old eight-inch layer of longitudinal timbers would have been difficult and costly to replace.

102.   In World War I there were extensive layouts of two-foot gauge railways behind the trenches to supply munitions and stores to the front lines. The FR tractors were of this origin. One of the US Alco 2-6-2Ts remained working in France at Pithiviers, from where it was purchased by John Ransom in 1964. After storage in London, he donated it to the FR where it arrived on 16th October. (A.G.W.Garraway)

103.   John Ransom and FR Driver Roy Goldstraw took the Alco for a trial trip on 4th November. Note that the cab had undergone surgery to suit the FR loading gauge. Its appearance was later altered drastically to meet FR requirements. (A.G.W.Garraway)

NEWS FROM THE LINE - Summer 1967

Traffic

Forecasts made at this stage of the operating season can too easily be proved rash even before they appear in print, but there is certainly no reason to suppose from the early season figures that 1967 will not be yet another record year. Easter fell early this year, but traffic was as good as ever, and the Sunday brought record crowds and a ten-coach double-headed train.

A.G.M. day was spoilt by continuous rain from mid-morning onwards, which was particularly unfortunate as modern power brought the BR special in well over an hour earlier than usual and there was time for a really leisurely and comfortable afternoon on the F.R. Both the morning train (eight coaches behind *Earl of Merioneth*) and the afternoon one (twelve with *Linda* and *Blanche*) ran through to Garnedd (West) before reversing to Tan-y-Bwlch, giving a total of some four hundred members their first journeys above Tan-y-Bwlch, albeit short ones with the scenery hidden in mist and cloud.

The next event of note was on Saturday, 6th May, when a special was run for the organisers of the Maid Marian Locomotive Fund. The morning had been spent at Dinorwic Quarries, Llanberis, where *Maid Marian* was ceremoniously handed over to the Fund, then the party of contributors made their way to Portmadoc and spent some time admiring station pilot *Britomart* before boarding their *Linda*-hauled train. High teas were served to fifty at Garnedd West, after which a meeting and discussion on *Maid Marion*'s future took place in a rather crowded buffet car.

The Spring Bank Holiday week started with a flourish. In anticipation of heavy traffic the full summer service of four trains was advertised for the Sunday, but even that proved insufficient. The 2.30 left at 2.10 with every seat taken, and then the timetable was abandoned and trains ran up and down as quickly as the guards could get them ready. The final tally was five extra trains and record figures for a Sunday. Tuesday also was exceptionally busy, with 1,402 bookings, but other days were too hot for record breaking and the final total for the week was very similar to last year's Whit week. That can be considered very satisfactory, as we have already had Whit week thrown in as a bonus this year.

Boston Lodge

Earl of Merioneth was ready for service at Easter, and double-headed the 2.30 on the Sunday with *Blanche*. The Fairlie was leaking steam from both steam chests, and after three or four more trips on light passenger and heavier works trains during Easter week, was taken into shops for further attention. The top bogie was dealt with by A.G.M. day and the bottom one during the following fortnight; in the latter case the steam chest was removed completely from the cylinders to permit an awkward flaw to be repaired. The leaks had nothing to do with the new flexible steam pipes, which appear to be doing their job well, in fact it was the lack of leaking steam from these that drew attention to the existence of the other leaks.

Linda's driving wheels were received back from the Hunslet Engine Co. at the end of March and she was soon back in service, at which stage *Blanche* was taken in for attention to a cracked cylinder which had manifested itself disturbingly. *Prince* passed a boiler inspection early in May following some repairs, and reassembly started immediately. By July the locomotive situation should be at its desirable level, with a Fairlie for heavy trains, *Linda* and *Blanche* for the medium duties and *Prince* for the lightweight evening trains and perhaps one of the morning trips.

Assembly of new coach No. 106 commenced at Easter and if all goes well it may enter service before the end of the season. It is a straightforward third-first-third saloon coach to the standard design. Incidentally, it may have been noticed that all new coaches are being numbered in the series started by No. 100, the observation car that entered service during the Passenger Centenary year. No. 24 has been renumbered 104, whilst 25 became 105 before it was finished. No. 101 will be another observation car, similar to 100 except that it will have guard's accommodation, whilst 103 will be a new buffet car, to be built next winter in time for the three-train Dduallt peak service. To leave the 1xx series clear and to avoid duplication of wagon and carriage numbers, three-ton slate wagons are being renumbered in the 3xx series and other low-numbered wagons are also being renumbered.

Bow-sider No. 20 left Portmadoc goods shed on 15th May after bodywork overhaul by the local joiners, and entered the paint shop. By that date No. 22 had been gutted prior to the fitting of its steel frame.

Permanent Way

The rather specialised relaying at Portmadoc was completed by Easter and the spotlight shifted once again to the Tan-y-Bwlch—Dduallt section. Easter weekend saw a magnificent volunteer effort, with the deturfing, ditching and cutting drainage being taken from Old Coed-y-Bleiddiau curve through to beyond Dduallt Manor. For most of the weekend there were no less than eighty volunteers working above Tan-y-Bwlch, the numbers being shared between P.W. and S. & T. departments and the deviation. The ditching was hastened by the willingness of the S. & T. linesmen (and women) to join in the digging when working ahead of their own programme (with, we would add, the full approval of their Union—*JASPER*). The Wickham trolley ran a frequent service between Tan-y-Bwlch and the working sites, often loaded with almost impossible numbers of volunteers and their equipment, ranging from ladders and drums of wire to the inevitable dozens of shovels. It clocked up over 100 valiant miles before limping back to Boston Lodge with a cracked wheel.

Rails, sleepers and chairs were then loaded up at Minffordd, and on the Friday after Easter, *Earl of Merioneth* took a massive 62-axle train up to Tan-y-Bwlch, whence Simplex took it over—in sections—for materials to be off-loaded in position, almost to Dduallt P.W. hut. A token section of twenty rail-lengths was then relaid, but after A.G.M. day, with trains running on Wednesdays only, attention shifted back below Tan-y-Bwlch. Twenty-five lengths at Pen-y-Bryn, for long a source of annoyance to the maintenance gang, had already been relaid by dint of 6.00 a.m.-2.00 p.m. shifts on two April weekends (all credit to the volunteer who was there from the start on all four days) and then work started on another bad stretch—Bryn Mawr. Here fifty-five lengths were resleepered in about nine working days, thanks in particular to a very productive weekend—29th-30th April—when small but very energetic working parties were present from three Groups.

These two lengths then had to be ballasted and tamped—under traffic in the case of Bryn Mawr, involving more early starts. Then came the Spring Bank Holiday, with the focus turning once again to the northern territories—and staying there, we hope, for many months to come, provided Will Jones and Fred Howes can keep pace with the maintenance work necessary on the lower sections.

Permanent Way Supplies

Until recently, the F.R. has automatically bought its sleepers and ballast from BR, but during the last four years it has been becoming increasingly difficult to get any sleepers of reasonable quality whilst spent ballast has tended to include the entire track formation, with small amounts of genuine ballast mixed with earth, clay and rocks. Somewhat reluctantly, other sources of supply have now been found. Sleepers are being purchased from the contractors who lift closed BR lines; most of those used between Tan-y-Bwlch and Coed-y-Bleiddiau came from a branch near Rochdale, whilst, after a crisis early this year, we have now obtained good supplies of ex-Great Central line timbers from Nottingham and Banbury. 1,400 were delivered in March and April, 330 at a time, on massive articulated lorries which could only get into Minffordd yard after part of the wall by the weigh-house had been demolished. One driver spent the night in Portmadoc before making his way

to Minffordd for unloading, but was misdirected over the top of the Cob and spent an unhappy two hours reversing his "bender" and its twenty-ton load back to Portmadoc.

Ballast is being purchased new from Minffordd Granite Quarry. The quarry's lorries tip it straight down the ballast chute into the ex-R.A.F. Hudson wagons. Some shovelling is still required, but forty tons or more can be handled quite easily in a day—a vast improvement on previous methods.

Some notes on costs might not be out of place. Sleepers are about 10s. each, so that each F.R. one costs a basic 5s. plus transport, and the labour of handling and cutting. The ballast costs about 21s. per ton delivered. In all cases quotations for delivery by rail have been more than double those of road transport. 4,000 sleepers are being put in between Tan-y-Bwlch and Dduallt; some 700 tons of ballast will be needed for tamping alone between Coed-y-Bleiddiau and Dduallt, whilst a further 1,000 tons will be used when we can afford the luxury of "topping-up". New chair screws, fishplate bolts and keys all add to the budget. Relaying a railway is an expensive business even when volunteers help to keep the labour costs down.

P.W.I. Visit

The Festiniog Railway and, in particular, its P.W. Dept. was "at home" on Monday, 22nd May, to the Permanent Way Institution. A gathering of about two hundred members of the Institution and their families was at Llandudno for their annual dinner and get-together, and of the optional excursions offered, the visit to the F.R. was the most popular. Four coach loads, totalling 138 people, arrived at mid-day and joined their special train with its full buffet facilities. The first stop was at Minffordd weigh-house, where most of the gentlemen braved a shower to examine a display of F.R. track and equipment in the exchange yard; they seemed impressed with the length of bull-head track laid down as an example of the present day relaying technique. Other equipment on show included the rail-mounted diesel generator with tamping hammers and screwing drills, Thermit welding apparatus, the weedkiller spraying wagon with pump and hand lances, and examples of the converted main line flange lubricators which are being used on the longer sharp bull-head curves.

On, then, to Tan-y-Bwlch, where *Blanche* took water and ran round the train, to propel it on to Garnedd (West) while the 2.30 was coming up behind *Earl of Merioneth*. When the passenger train had arrived, the special ran down through the station and the two train sets were joined to form a very spacious 3.35 down—the second twelve-coacher of the year. The efficient way in which this manoeuvre was handled was duly noted by the P.W.I. party before they made their way down the station approach to their waiting coaches.

An overflow party of fifty-five came over from Llandudno two days later, to travel in reserved coaches in the service train. There is no doubt that during the two visits the F.R. made many new friends—and potentially very useful ones, too.

104. The south end of Harbour station was cut back in December 1959 to permit the construction of a new road for the conveyance of power station components to be unloaded from ships. The road was not laid as another wharf was used. This December photograph includes the Guide Hut which was situated in the car park for many years. (A.G.W.Garraway)

NEWS FROM THE LINE - Autumn 1967

Traffic

"The passenger explosion" is how the General Manager (normally phlegmatic where traffic figures are concerned) has been heard to describe this year's peak season, and we can offer no better analogy, even though most of the debris has been swept into litter bins. In 1966 we described the 1,863 bookings recorded on 17th August as "staggering". By that date this year we were not being staggered by anything under 2,000 on a weekday. The peak came later—on 30th August—with 2,350 bookings, corresponding to something like 4,790 single passenger journeys if pre-booked coach parties are counted in.

Consistent weather conditions without extremes of sunshine or rain throughout August resulted in the weekly figures being even more impressive than the daily ones. The old record of 14,476 passenger journeys in a week was broken in five consecutive weeks, with 16,801 in week ending 5th August, 17,457 on the 12th, 17,933 on the 19th, 19,881 on the 26th and 20,451 on 2nd September—an incredible sequence which must obviously owe something to the TV broadcast on 18th August. With last year's total being passed as early as 26th August and exceptionally good results being recorded during early September, the final figures will be well in excess of 210,000. By the middle of September the journey figure for bookings on the line had reached the 200,000 mark.

Coping with passengers in these greatly increased numbers has not been easy. On at least a dozen days during August every train from the 12-5 to the 4-35 was filled to capacity; on Wednesdays and Thursdays, with a boost from Butlins. the morning trains also often ran full. Rarely were there any spare coaches at Portmadoc before 5-00 p.m. The "A" train set was used on the 10-40 1-20 and 3-10 departures, Monday to Thursday, generally with seven bogies, and the 5-45 and 7-30 with five or six, while the "B" set worked the 10-10, 12-5, 2-30 and 4-35 with a maximum of seven bogies and the four-wheelers. On Fridays, with no evening trains, the workings were reversed, and at weekends the workings were so arranged to permit servicing of both train sets.

The locomotive roster was as regular as clockwork. *Prince* was entrusted with the two evening trips and, on Mondays, Tuesdays and Fridays, the 10-10; *Blanche* took the 10-40 and 3-10; *Linda* had the 1-20 and 4-35 and also the 10-10 on "Butlin" days; *Earl of Merioneth* toyed with the heaviest trains at 12-5 and 2-30. Timekeeping was again of the highest order, for the careful rostering ensured that there was virtually no overloading of locomotives; the hardest turn of most days was *Linda's* 4-35, which often had seven bogies and the four-wheelers.

Although by far the quietest day of the week, the Saturday timetable, with only one train set in use, provided the operating highlights. As early as 3rd June, the 2-30 had to be made up to ten bogies, *Linda* handing over to *Earl* at Pen Cob due to damp conditions, and on 19th August *Linda* toiled up unassisted with nine. A week later came the long-awaited opportunity to see what a Fairlie in good condition could really do, for the 2-30 required twelve bogies to carry 407 passengers. There were three lengthy stops *en route* while still more passengers were crammed in, and in starting from Penrhyn *Earl* strained a steam-pipe joint which had to be nursed thereafter. Even so, Evan Davies had the train at Tan-y-Bwlch within forty minutes after leaving Portmadoc.

The only instance of really late running was on Wednesday, 16th August, when an early morning P.W. train from Tan-y-Bwlch to Minffordd was delayed in section with a broken axle. The 10-10 only ran to Minffordd and the 10-40 was almost an hour late; on the way down it passed the 12-5 up (also late) at Penrhyn, this being the first time the lengthened loop has been used to pass two scheduled passenger trains, and things were back to normal by the afternoon. The day's bookings figure of 1,833 gives little indication of the operating problems that were overcome.

Traffic receipts, of course, have shown an equally healthy trend throughout the summer, with first-class patronage being increased when accommodation would allow. The Sales Department, under Maurice Bolton's leadership, has greatly extended its scope at Portmadoc, with a tea bar being opened in the Museum and a light refreshment counter in the booking hall, to leave the main shop free to exhibit a greater range of literature and souvenirs.

Boston Lodge

Once *Prince* had re-entered service towards the end of June there were only minor jobs to be done on the steam locomotives in service, although these occasionally required some late night or early morning sessions to have them ready for their rostered duties. The Simplex diesel *Mary Ann* received some attention during July, and was later equipped with vacuum pipes and brake valve to enable her to run attached to a passenger train down from Tan-y-Bwlch after a day on P.W. duties.

Britomart has continued to appear on light non-passenger duties from time to time, and has ventured as far as Garnedd by using a pump to replenish her tanks at Gysgfa.

A great effort was made on coach No. 22, with Fred Boughey and his volunteer gang joining forces with joinery contractor Idris Williams and painter Tommy Morgan. The coach was back in service on 8th August in varnished livery and minus sag, but had to return to the works on two or three evenings for its upholstered seating to be fitted.

Work was then stepped up on the new saloon coach, No. 106, which has now reached the fitting-out stage. It will not see passenger service this year, but will soon be moved out of the erecting bay to leave room to start on the main coach-building job for the winter—the new buffet car. The prefabricated sections for this arrived at Boston Lodge during July; it is to be a superlative job, embodying many new features and ideas resulting from the lessons learned in operating the present buffet cars, and designed with the limited resources of Dduallt station very much in mind. It is also planned to complete the rebuild of coach No. 16 before next summer, making a minimum of 17 bogie coaches available for the peak service.

More work has been done recently on the long-term extension of facilities at Boston Lodge. The new shed in Glanymor has been roofed, and doors are being fitted. It will provide covered accommodation for stock this winter, and work has started on the extension of the long road of the locomotive shed through into the new building.

Permanent Way

The "construction gang", with from two to four permanent staff and any number of volunteers, have been above Tan-y-Bwlch almost every day since early July, with very satisfactory results. By mid-September, relaying was within 300 yards of the planned site for the bottom points of Dduallt station and a start had been made on the formidable amount of ballasting and packing that has to be done. Evie Roberts, assisted by Tom Davies (when not driving) and volunteers, has made great strides with the fencing, but much remains to be done.

The two-man maintenance crew can also be well satisfied with their summer's work; the fact that they have not had to spend an undue length of time at any one location but have remained mobile and able to attend to any minor troubles as they arise is perhaps indicative of the improving overall standard of the track. The Cob, however, continues to require more than its share of attention.

Signals and Telegraph

The department had a week's excursion to Corwen in mid-July, where they dismantled large quantities of B.R. signalling equipment, including two lever frames and four signal posts, prior to the Llangollen—Bala line being handed over to the demolition contractors. The equipment was transported to Boston Lodge on the F.R. Company's lorry, and overhaul of some of the items has begun. With the exception of actual signal posts, several more of which will eventually be needed, the exercise has provided the F.R. with enough equipment to signal all its existing stations.

Deviation News

At a speed varying between one and five feet per week, the embankment at Site 1 is slowly but surely creeping out towards the now static Site 2. Four sites are being dug: the main quarry at the top end of the station, Site 0 halfway down, Site -1 at the bottom end and, nearing completion, clearance of debris following blasting for the abutments of the bridge over the cutting. Temporary track has been laid as a continuation of the station siding, slewed outwards, and only a few feet of rock prevent a connection with one of the quarry sidings. When joined, this will permit two-way skip traffic through the station and eliminate some of the congestion that arises when all Sites are being worked simultaneously.

During August, the 1967 Ffestergraph output passed the 1966 total figure, and by the end of the month 1,769 truckloads had been shifted. In addition to regular weekend parties, digging has been carried on by smaller holiday groups throughout much of the summer.

1968

NEWS FROM THE LINE - Winter 1968

Traffic

A remarkably satisfactory season finally ended on 5th November, a little ignominiously perhaps, when it was decided that 25 passengers did not justify any further extension of the operating season. The previous Sunday, with no publicity but better weather, about 60 passengers had turned up. The extra trains run at week-ends during October contributed very nearly 1,000 passenger journeys towards the total for the year, which is expected to reach 220,000 when all the results are to hand from B.R. and coach operators.

September brought no notable operating highlights, but consistently increased passenger figures were recorded throughout; the 2.30 required eight bogies as late as 27th September.

The coach mileage recorded during the season rose by 20% to just over 78,400. The main train observation and buffet cars each covered 7,938 miles and the two standard saloons just a few miles less. Bow-sider No. 18, overhauled during the winter, was next in the table with 5,221 miles, whilst all told no less than thirteen bogie coaches exceeded the 3,500 mark. The bug-boxes each travelled 1,527 miles, 50% up on last year. The train mileage was about 11,700, making the *average* train equivalent to very nearly seven bogie coaches.

A traffic census was made during a week in July, mainly to ascertain whether there have been any changes in traffic trends since the last census which would influence services to Dduallt. The results were very much as expected, but some details may be of interest. Six hundred and ten forms were completed, representing 2,386 passengers, 81% of whom were visiting the Railway for the first time. About 85% had come by private car, together, no doubt, with many of the 4% who were staying in Portmadoc. Seventy-five per cent had come to Portmadoc especially to visit the Railway. Of the reasons which prompted the visit, 20% had been told of the Railway by friends, 17% had seen it advertised in local guide books, etc., and 16% had read about it in magazines and periodicals. Only 6% said they had just come across the Railway by accident, this being a surprisingly low figure. However, 40% had turned up without having seen a timetable.

Significantly, 94% of the passengers said they would have travelled to Dduallt if the train had been going through, 3% had insufficient time and 3% felt it might have been too expensive. Eighty-seven per cent were completely satisfied with their journey, others made constructive suggestions of great diversity.

Boston Lodge

With the passenger coaches coming into the erecting shop, one after the other, for their annual overhaul of running gear, etc. none of the major winter jobs have been started yet, but a great number of minor tasks, varied even by Boston Lodge standards, have been accomplished. As far as loco-motives are concerned, a certain amount of effort has been put in on the Alco —detailed elsewhere—whilst *Merddin Emrys* has been partially stripped. *Blanche* has had her wheels out for axlebox attention and was in the erecting shop for work on the motion at the end of November.

Work has also been done on four diesel power units. E1, the P.W. generator, is being equipped with metal side and end plates to replace the existing canvas sheets; E2, a mobile alternator for the C.E.G. Tunnel Mess, has been almost totally enclosed and prepared for work in far from ideal conditions; A3 and A4, both air compressors, have been overhauled, for driving rock drills and breaking equipment at Dduallt and Garnedd Tunnel respectively. Colonel Campbell's spare Simplex has also been in the shop for spare-time work.

The new saloon coach was moved out of the erecting shop, mounted temporarily on the spare set of bogies (N.W.N.G. type, ex W.H.R. coach No. 21) to enable assembly work to start on the new buffet car. Most of the component parts for three pairs of bogies have been made. In the paint shop, coach No. 15 has been refinished in green and ivory livery. The seaward side, which had been deteriorating very rapidly, has been completely burnt off and repainted, whilst the other side only needed slight patching and revarnish-ing. Some of the coaches in varnished livery are being revarnished where necessary.

The Glan-y-Mor building programme has progressed sufficiently for the new building to be used for storage of rolling stock, in conditions which are dry, if not quite suitable for winter work. Works staff have assisted the S. & T. Dept. with the erection of the new Cob signal and will be getting increas-ingly involved with the work in Garnedd Tunnel as it progresses.

Permanent Way

With the exception of Garnedd Tunnel and the Dduallt Station area, basic relaying between Tan-y-Bwlch and Dduallt was completed on 24th October. The initial ballasting was then hurried along, to be finished in mid-November. That enabled the work of setting up the track level and shovel packing the ballast underneath the sleepers to proceed in earnest, with a target date for completion of the second week in January. The tamping hammers are being used on all joint sleepers, and some work on drainage, fishplate adjustment, etc. is being done concurrently.

The laying of 600 tons of ballast in under ten weeks was a noteworthy operation, making good use of the Group working parties available at week-ends. Each Thursday a series of lorries would bring 8¼-ton loads to Minffordd Exchange Sidings and tip the ballast down the chute into waiting wagons. A lorry load would fill three or four F.R. wagons and careful co-ordination was necessary to ensure that the right amount was tipped into each. The Sim-plex would then be used to shunt the loaded wagons up to the long siding and put more empties below the chute. Thirty tons per week was the initial order, but this was soon increased to sixty, making up a train of 22 or more wagons. On Friday or Saturday, *Prince* or *Linda* would work the train up to the section to be ballasted, *Prince* making two trips, *Linda* sometimes managing it in one, and the unloading would keep the week-end working parties occupied for most of Saturday, any spare time being used to load up the wagons with timber or materials left over from the relaying. The train would return to Minffordd whenever convenient—one notable return working is illustrated. During the last week in October, with volunteers from HANSAG present daily, the order was stepped up to sixty tons on alternate days—they won't forget "International Ballast Week"!

On 11th November, after a couple of preliminary visits, two skilled rockmen from Maenofferen Quarries, Blaenau Ffestiniog, started work in Garnedd Tunnel, removing projecting lumps of rock from the roof. They are working at week-ends, with the P.W. Dept. providing men to attend to the equipment—generator for lighting, compressor for rock drills, etc. When the roof is finished, Boston Lodge will be joining forces with P.W., tackling the sides and floor, and then the somewhat specialised relaying. In the mean-time, a temporary siding is being laid, outside the tunnel at the bottom end, to accommodate the variety of vehicles that will be needed at certain stages of the work and enable them to be shunted. By the time these notes are published it may be possible to estimate how long the tunnel work will take; at present nobody can even guess.

S. & T.

The Cob boasts a semaphore signal once again. Not, perhaps, as distinctive as the ill-fated trident, but certainly just as effective. It is a composite job, embracing the post from the old "W.H.R." signal near Portmadoc goods shed, rodding and other fittings from the trident, an arm from an old Liver-pool Overhead Railway signal, and a finial believed to be from an F.R. post at Blaenau. Improved interlocking ensures that the signal can only be pulled off when the road is set right through to the platform.

The permanent wiring between Tan-y-Bwlch and Dduallt has been steadily improved throughout 1967 and is only one wet week-end behind schedule.

Staff News

We are pleased to record that Bill Hoole continues to make progress following his illness last Easter, and has enjoyed many trips "on the cushions" as well as renewing his First World War acquaintance with an Alco's foot-plate. Our congratulations go to platelayer Fred Howes, whose engagement to Miss Margaret Roberts was announced in October.

Will and Bessie Jones are retiring early in 1968, and with the Works Dept. facing ever-increasing demands on their manpower some new names are expected to appear on the permanent roll-call in the near future. The first is expected to be Roy Goldstraw, who is already a familiar figure at Boston Lodge (latterly overhauling the running gear of coach 16), on the fireman's side of the Fairlies (he was the brow-mopper on the May sheet of the 1967 Calendar) and on T.V. (lucidly explaining why volunteers volunteer). Roy will be employed as a fitter/driver, and will be taking over the Alco in both capacities.

During the 1967 season, the opportunity was taken to train seasonal regulars and some newcomers in a greater range of duties, in anticipation of increased demands on operating staff when trains are running to Dduallt; two or three were added to the list of authorised junior guards and junior controller/booking clerks. The 1968 traffic staff roster will be taking shape by the time this is published; opportunities for training newcomers in the more responsible positions may be limited, but nevertheless new volunteers for traffic work, with a view to attaining possible "seasonal staff" status in due course, will be as welcome as ever. In particular there are vacancies on the commercial side for good and enthusiastic sales staff, behind shop counters and in the buffet cars. These are jobs where, generally, womenfolk shine more than the men. How about it, ladies?

There will certainly be vacancies for firemen in the 1968 season, as it is hoped to have more engines running than at any time since the 1930s, if not earlier. If inexperienced volunteers who aspire to engine work can arrange to come for a stay of a fortnight or more, there is a better chance to give some training and then use them more usefully in their second week. In this connection, an old friend of the Railway, Jim Maxwell, returned to the foot-plate in the 1967 season after an absence of some years, and performed a useful service instructing new and inexperienced firemen.

105. Work was well advanced at Dduallt in March and *Prince* arrived with a test train on the 30th, despite delays in the work due to travel restrictions owing to foot and mouth disease. The loop was not completed until 20th May. (A.G.W.Garraway)

NEWS FROM THE LINE - Spring 1968

Reopening to Dduallt

The restrictions necessarily imposed by the foot and mouth epidemic have seriously hampered the volunteer effort and particularly the work of the deviationists, who are quarrying into the hillside by Dduallt Station to make space for the run-round loop and thereby obtain fill for the first section of embankment.

The P.W. Dept., by dint of very hard work, have more or less completed the track-laying up to Dduallt Station, although there is still a lot to do in the way of filling up with ballast and, of course, the new track will need to be handled gently during a settling-in period. The quarry rock-men have completed their work in Garnedd Tunnel and the track-laying therein is now in progress. The Signal and Telegraph Department's work is well in hand.

The Railway Company have therefore announced that it is hoped to reopen to Dduallt on 6th April. However, a slight amendment to the timetable mentioned in the last *Magazine* will be necessary; as no full run-round facilities will be available initially at Dduallt, an engine will be kept there to take the train down to Tan-y-Bwlch, and in view of the amount of work which will still be in progress, passengers will not be detraining at Dduallt. Departure times from Portmadoc will not be affected.

Boston Lodge

The locomotive mileages for 1967 were as follows:—

Locomotive	1967 Season	Total under Present Administration
Prince	1,535	36,481
Merddin Emrys	nil	11,924
Earl of Merioneth	3,017	24.162
Linda	5,062	20,048
Blanche	3,673	9,058
The Alco	48	48
Moelwyn	803	17,249
Simplex Tractor	2,156	3,658
Wickham Trolley	2,739	7,496
Tyke	nil	180

Roy Goldstraw started work on 1st January as fitter-driver, and is being allocated the Alco as his pride and joy. Conversion to left-hand drive is now virtually complete and work is well in hand on other necessary jobs; the motion is being given as much attention as possible and vacuum brake is being fitted. The boiler is being retubed, the Boiler Inspector having been well satisfied with the state of the (1917) boiler barrel, which has a remarkably "as new" appearance. The Alco's compensated springing makes alteration to the weight distribution very difficult, but the compensation arrangements to the pony trucks have alternative settings; they will be altered to give maximum adhesion.

Earl of Merioneth, Blanche and *Linda* are all ready for a season's very hard work. Stripping of *Merddin Emrys*'s lagging has revealed a fracture in the middle ring, top end, which it would not be practicable to repair, bearing in mind the age of the boiler. This means that renewal becomes a matter of more immediate importance and both the Company and Society are giving considerable thought to all the problems involved.

Upnor Castle arrived on 13th February. Conversion to Festiniog gauge is not considered a formidable job and is being given priority. Another newly-arrived piece of machinery is a Matisa self-propelled ballast tamping machine.

Its conversion to "2 ft." gauge, though basically quite simple, will involve much more work.

The winter has not seen a great deal of progress on coach body construction, due to the foot and mouth restriction, but some work has been done on the new saloon No. 106 and 96-year-old No. 16. The frame of buffet car No. 103 is ready for assembly of the body to commence. Thanks to the mass-production of six sets of parts, bogies for the new coaches can be put together within a few days as and when required. Those for No. 106 are already available.

Following the death last autumn of the sitting tenant, Miss Langsdale, the cottage at Boston Lodge near the top of the toll-gate steps has become available for Railway use, and is to be refurbished for occupation by permanent staff. The adjacent cottage is, of course, occupied by Bill and Dolly Hoole.

The Company's lorry visited Portmadoc on 17-18th February—the first trip for some time. The outward load consisted of a great variety of materials, including S. & T. materials and metal staff lockers; on the return trip *Upnor Castle*'s wheels, for regauging, formed the cargo.

Permanent Way

If P.W. work consisted solely of track work, we could record a very satisfactory winter's achievement. The track from the top end of Garnedd Tunnel to the bottom of Dduallt Station is ready for passenger traffic, although a few days spent re-aligning curves and adjusting fishplates will enhance its appearance and riding qualities as time permits. At Dduallt, the bottom points have been relaid in their new position and the old main line relaid as far as the start of the new embankment; some ballast and packing is needed after which the station will be usable for passenger trains with the assistance of a station pilot. The laying of the points at the top end and the completion of the run-round loop will take place later in the spring, after the deviationists have had a chance to make up for time lost during the winter, so that the loop can be put in without disturbing the trees and shrubs which make Dduallt so attractive.

At Tan-y-Bwlch the re-alignment of the top points and the down road through the station is complete, and a catch point has been installed at the top end of the up line. The up line still has to be moved to its new position to give adequate room for the island platform, but this job is being saved for Easter to make use of the good turn-out of volunteers always present on that week-end. A week's concentrated work titivating the "Army" section along Tafarntrip will bring that more-or-less up to standard.

That leaves us with just one problem: Garnedd Tunnel. Since early November, Wynne and Dai, the two skilled rock-men from Blaenau, have spent most Saturdays and Sundays scraping, chipping, drilling and blasting at the roof and sides of the tunnel, not only enlarging it, but using their skill and experience to leave it safe and free from the risk of falls. It has been an awkward job, complicated by the poor quality and mixed strata of the rock at each end, and it was not until 17th February that bogie wagon No. 63, equipped with a specially-made structure gauge template would run through without touching somewhere. It is still necessary to lower the floor under the portals, where clearance is narrowest, and to remove some projecting rock from the floor and drainage cesses in other places. Just how long this will take remains to be seen, but it must be done before relaying can be completed. The track in the tunnel itself is to be laid in one long-welded length, involving the Thermit welding of about 22 joints, and the whole job requires great precision in rather uncomfortable conditions.

As far as the P.W. is concerned, if trains can get through the tunnel on 6th April, they can go through to Dduallt.

106. No, not a party of wealthy passengers, but a Rolls Royce enthusiasts' event on 24th May. Such people have an affinity with railway volunteers and like to include visits to such heritage attractions in their rallies. (A.G.W.Garraway)

NEWS FROM THE LINE - Summer 1968

Traffic

There was no grand opening ceremony—not even a peal of bells—but "Dd. Day"—6th April—was a memorable one for all that. As *Earl of Merioneth* eased her nine-coach train over Tan-y-Bwlch top points a new stage in the Festiniog Railway's history was beginning—a stage which, during the first month at any rate, was to attract well over 50% more passengers and to enthral them with the magnificent scenery of the Dduallt run.

A great deal was learned on that first week-end, and by Easter most of the snags had been ironed out and the somewhat complicated operating procedures had become routine, so that the unprecedented volume of bank holiday traffic was handled quite efficiently. An accurate forecast of traffic requirements had been made during the previous week, and the special time-table of four trains on the Saturday and Sunday and five on Monday proved to be just sufficient. Fortunately, the Traffic Dept. was strongly manned and most trains had two or three guards gaining valuable experience of holiday traffic.

This state of affairs did not last long, however, and with three engines being required in steam daily (train engine, Dduallt pilot, spare) the usual early-season shortage of mid-week volunteers became critical. On one May Wednesday the P.W. Dept. had to provide guard, buffet attendant and two enginemen—even ganger Ron Lester took a turn at firing *Prince*—and the Works Dept. were no better off.

A feature of the season has been the mileage already clocked by *Earl of Merioneth*. Afternoon trains have been consistently loading to at least seven bogies and only the Fairlie is really able to cope with these loads on this year's timings with the early-season rusty rails. This problem will recede as the season progresses, of course, and in the peak season the size of trains will tend to be limited by the number of coaches available for the three train sets. Nevertheless, it is anticipated that the Fairlie will not be spending very many days on shed this summer, highlighting the pressing need for more big engines.

The daily routine on week-day operating days during April and early May has invariably opened with *Prince* running light to Dduallt, sometimes being commandeered for P.W. ballast or shunting duties but always being positioned in the bottom end of the incompleted loop at Dduallt by 11.20. On arrival of the train, *Prince* would be coupled to the bottom end, the train engine would be uncoupled and the train would leave, sometimes after a stay of less than two minutes. At Tan-y-Bwlch, *Prince* would run into the bottom siding and the train engine would hurry down light from Dduallt on receiving clearance from Control, to run through the loop at Tan-y-Bwlch and couple to the train for the resumed journey to Portmadoc. That would leave *Prince* free for P.W. duties for a couple of hours and then the same procedure would be followed for the afternoon train except that on most days *Prince* would take the train through to Portmadoc—with eight coaches or more this could be quite an eyebrow-raising working—while the train engine followed

light or with a P.W. train. Over Easter, with the more intensive service, the loco of each up train worked down through to Portmadoc with the following train—a system which caused excitement among young—and old—passengers, with four different engines to be "spotted".

A.G.M. day saw all available coaching stock in service, with *Earl* and *Blanche* sharing the main honours. The first rain for a week fell just as *Earl* made a vociferous entry into Dduallt with the main train and continued until the evening meetings were getting under way, but otherwise all arrangements went like clockwork. Other noteworthy days were 1st May, when hot chicken dinners were served to thirty-six Penrhyn residents on a privately chartered evening special, 15th May, when coach parties boosted the afternoon train to eleven bogies, hauled (for the most part through thick mist) by *Earl* and *Blanche*, and 23rd May, when the Railway was honoured to have as passengers from Minffordd to Tan-y-Bwlch on a special train Dr. Hastings Banda, President of Malawi, and Lord Snowdon.

By 20th May the loop at Dduallt had been completed and *Prince*'s daily "Dduallt South End Pilot" special duty came to an end. In general, the "ZZ Timetable", as it was inevitably called, had worked well and traffic staff had been amazed by the high proportion of passengers who seemed to know just what was happening and why. On quieter days, the water stop at Tan-y-Bwlch would be quite sufficient for traffic requirements in the up direction, the turn-round at Dduallt would only be a matter of two or three minutes, and a leisurely fifteen minute stop at Tan-y-Bwlch helped buffet and shop sales and gave husbands time to photograph both engines while wives hunted in vain for the Welsh lady. On busy days, however, the number of passengers leaving and joining the train at Tan-y-Bwlch on the way up provided a considerable challenge to efficient operating, and guards found themselves welcoming the single-journey coach parties that would leave compartments free for passengers making the short return trip to Dduallt. The crossing of trains and the handling of passengers at Tan-y-Bwlch have been the subjects of much speculative discussion ever since the reopening to Dduallt has been in sight, and the indications are that this apprehension is going to be fully justified when things get really busy.

Boston Lodge

Before 6th April the accent was on helping the P.W. and S. & T. Depts. to complete essential work for the reopening, since when the operating of train services has inevitably slowed down the tempo of work, with routine maintenance always to be done on engines and coaches as well as the provision of actual crews. For once the season commenced with all four locomotives ready for traffic and they were necessary over Easter.

Roy Goldstraw continues the overhaul and modifications to his special charge—the Alco—with assistance from others from time to time. The boiler work has been held up until suitable stay taps could be borrowed from Vulcan

107. With Tan-y-bwlch becoming an important crossing place for trains, it had to be relaid and upgraded in May. The island platform soon followed and the goods shed, in the background, became a refreshment room. (A.G.W.Garraway)

Foundry. David Baskcomb has concentrated on *Upnor Castle*'s modifications, chiefly entailing reducing the cab to its original height. (It had obviously been raised during manufacture, probably as a result of a visit from some Admiralty tall brass, as evidenced by various holes and slots for doors, etc.) A rotary exhauster, rusted solid, obtained from an overturned gulley emptier, yielded to Boston Lodge pressure and proved to be of a type suitable for vacuum brake operation. It has been mounted and tested, and found to be as effective as, if not more so than, the steam locomotives' ejectors. Proportional equipment from a scrapped 204 h.p. B.R. diesel will complete this aspect of the work. The wheels are expected back from regauging towards the end of May.

The conversion of the Matisa tamper to F.R. gauge makes slow but steady progress under the charge of one of the regular Boston Lodge volunteers.

Work on the three new coaches continues. Saloon No. 106 is nearing completion; the Restaurant Car No. 103 is assembled, and fitting out, mostly by contractors, is well advanced; the underframe for Observation Car No. 101 (similar to 100) is being assembled. Four bogies have been made and completion of the remainder will not be a long task with all the components "mass produced".

No. 9, the van ex W. & L. (previously V. of R.) was returned from Bletchley on A.G.M. week-end resplendent in sprayed maroon livery with bilingual notes. With vacuum train pipe it can, like bogie open 63, run in passenger trains, and will be of use in carrying materials under cover, avoiding the necessity for special works trains. It is a very useful piece of equipment, even if not in daily use, and joins the list of successfully completed homework projects.

As a result of seeing an article on the Deviation by D. H. Wilson in a "Country Life" for November, 1967, Mr. H. A. Bierrum of the Civil Engineering firm of that name very kindly offered the Railway a 2¾ ton Ruston & Hornsby DL type 11-13 h.p. diesel, with a Ruston V.T.O. engine. This loco was built in 1939, works No. 201970, and went to Bierrum's in 1949. It was cleaned up and painted before being delivered to Minffordd on one of Bierrum's lorries, and carries the name "*Alistair*". At present it is chiefly used by Boston Lodge for personnel transport, but as the deviation work expands it will be useful for its intended purpose.

Permanent Way

When the last Magazine went to press, work was about to start on digging out the floor of Garnedd Tunnel prior to relaying. The digging proved an even more formidable job than expected; the soft top surface had oddly expansive qualities when broken up and a day's digging would often produce very little noticeable result, whilst the rock underneath was exceptionally hard and could only be loosened by blasting; a great deal of energy was expended in gaining a lowering of rail level of only an inch or two, although a satisfactory drop of three or four inches was accomplished in the portals where the clearances were critical. Additional digging was necessary to accommodate slotted plastic drain pipes which run continuously along the centre of the tunnel, well below sleeper level. Eventually, the track was laid and welding completed. Final levelling, packing and ballasting were completed only two days before the M.o.T. inspection on Sunday, 31st March.

On the Saturday, *Prince* ran through to Dduallt with a clearance train—the first time coach No. 100 had ventured east of Garnedd—and on the Sunday the P.W. staff and volunteers were working on Dduallt loop, with little to indicate to Colonel Robertson how much sweat had been expended twelve hours a day and seven days a week so that things were ready for his inspection and could be seen to be suitable for public services a week later.

The Colonel's departure was followed by icy winds, sleet and snow, some of which was still lying when *Earl of Merioneth* arrived at Dduallt with a bug-box and seven bogies on a test train on Thursday, 4th April; it was not until the four-wheeler was safely standing at Dduallt that the relaying could really be said to be complete, as these vehicles can easily foul in places that a bogie coach would clear. Ballast was laid on the main line in Dduallt station on the Friday and setting up and packing was done on Saturday morning; by lunchtime a six-coach train could be accommodated, volunteers took staggered lunches to keep the packing going and at 14.00 there was room for eight coaches. Finally, when the nine-coach train arrived there was actually room for ten—but it was too close for comfort!

With such an intensive work programme at Dduallt and other key locations there was little time to prepare for the squads of volunteers arriving at Easter, but as on many other week-ends there was plenty of picking and shovelling to be done at Dduallt shoulder-to-shoulder with the deviationists, whilst numerous other jobs were done during the week-end, some of them on the list left by Colonel Robertson. After Easter, Colonel Campbell's Simplex was returned to him after being on loan to the P.W. Dept. for about three months. Being stationed above Garnedd when tunnel work was in progress and at Tan-y-Bwlch at other times it had performed an invaluable service, running hundreds of miles with personnel or works trains of great variety and, on occasions, considerable weight.

Since Easter, the loop at Dduallt has been extended, length by length, between the trees and the newly-worked rock face, with an exacting double curve at the top end to weave between the trees and join up with the main line on the old embankment. The loop was completed by 20th May, when the spotlight turned to Tan-y-Bwlch, where the up line still had to be relaid in its new position to create the badly-needed island platform and the down-line catch point was high on the priority list.

Signals and Telegraphs

The busiest period in the department's history saw the winter's arrears overcome, though with very little time to spare. Boston Lodge staff joined forces with the volunteer pointfitters' gang, who had taken special leave, to complete the rodding of the top end of Tan-y-Bwlch Station only minutes before the first train on 6th April, whilst the final adjustments at Dduallt bottom point and catch point were completed during Easter week.

The omnibus telephone circuit was reinstated to Dduallt in good time for Dd. Day, and a temporary version of the automatic system was made available at Easter. Installation of the electric train staff equipment has proceeded steadily on S. & T. week-ends. Colonel Campbell has been spending his spare time building a hut to house his staff instrument; it rather shames the No. 1 van body which temporarily serves the same purpose at Dduallt Station.

108. On 1st December, the ex-GWR crane was used to load the bottom bogie from *Merddin Emrys* for transport to the Hunslet Engine Co., Leeds. The ex-wool merchant's Leyland Beaver had been assembled in 1946 from wartime spares and was to a design from the 1930s. (A.G.W.Garraway)

109. The north portal of the old Moelwyn Tunnel was recorded with the water near its maximum level. The remaining stonework gradually vanished. (N.F.Gurley coll.)

NEWS FROM THE LINE - Autumn 1968

Traffic

The early season results were so spectacular up to the end of June that the more recent figures, satisfactory though they are, form something of an anti-climax. Every week in June recorded an increase in traffic over the similar week in 1967 of 50% or more, but by these standards July was a poor month with the third week actually only just beating the same week in 1967. Then with the start of the peak season things picked up again and the news was made not so much by the numbers of passengers as by the tremendous efforts made to carry them.

It will be appreciated that the 1968 timetable was devised with a certain number of locomotives and coaches in view. Due to many setbacks, including of course the foot and mouth epidemic, the rolling stock available has been two coaches (Nos. 101 and 16) and one locomotive (the Alco) short of expectations. The carrying capacity of 16 and the pulling power of the Alco have been missed to an extent that has caused one headache after another since the first day of the three-train peak service. Fortunately, the Boiler Inspector allowed *Prince* to run the full season (after a special hydraulic test) but the run-down condition of the engine, coupled with tight timings and loads a little too near *Prince*'s limit, presented many problems. Nevertheless, with good enginemanship, *Prince* has given the occasional good performance in unfavourable conditions, proving more than ever that running these engines needs experienced crews.

To add to the other difficulties, a coal and water crisis developed early in August. When the collieries were on holiday a load of particularly bad coal, probably from a stock dump, came in, and all the engines promptly developed steaming troubles. At the same time (and readers from the South of England may find this hard to believe) virtually no rain fell in the area for five weeks. The water-course feeding Tan-y-Bwlch tanks—normally a healthy stream and sometimes a raging torrent—all but dried up, taking all night and part of the morning to replenish the tanks. The station house's supply completely disappeared for several weeks and almost every train carried supplies of drinking water for the house and cafe. The old slate tank by Campbell's Platform—the supply to which has never been known to fail—was being hastily reinstated for emergency use, but fortunately the rains came and averted the crisis. Never has good heavy rain been so welcome at Portmadoc!

It had been ascertained during Spring Bank Holiday week, firstly that the advertised service would be inadequate on busy days and secondly that with good locomotive performances and trains crossing at Penrhyn instead of Minffordd a 45-minute regular interval service could be maintained. A revised timetable was therefore drawn up with a 45-minute service operating between 14.00 and 17.45, the morning and evening trains being as advertised, and this was introduced on Mondays to Thursdays from early August until 4th September. This timetable had the great value of giving the bulk-carrying train

three mid-day-peak trips (11.30, 14.00 and 16.15) whereas the published timetable had its third trip leaving at 16.50—too late for many people. (The travelling public would, to our eternal regret, happily queue for hours early in the afternoon, but is as reluctant as ever to undertake a journey that ends after 18.15.)

This timetable was known, behind the scenes, as the "half panic". A "full panic" one was also available, with a first departure at 9.45 and then at 45-minute intervals from 10.15, giving a total of 13 return trips during the day. This was tried on 31st July, but a slight shower in the woods during the afternoon completely floored *Prince*, who had earlier had a struggle with a six-coach train, and as this put the service back by 45 minutes one train was lost. Three weeks later, on 21st August, good crowds on top of exceptionally heavy coach party bookings necessitated the introduction of the 45-minute service after the 10.00 and 10.40 had left early with every seat taken, and the maximum 13 trains were successfully run.

There was a certain amount of juggling with the carriage set workings and locomotive rosters, to endeavour to minimise the difficulties, and by the end of August a reasonably satisfactory arrangement had been evolved. Adroit use of Penrhyn loop on occasions during the morning also helped, allowing time lost by *Prince* on his first up trip to be minimised before the afternoon peak, and conversely one or two afternoon crossings at Minffordd instead of Penrhyn also helped to speed things up. Control really had to live up to its name, and the traffic and locomotive staffs had to keep right on their toes, with absolutely no reserves.

Expressing all this in terms of figures, the weekly passenger journey totals, discounting pre-booked parties, for the seven weeks of the peak service, were 17,138, 21,229, 22,868, 22,580, 21,279, 23,976 and 17,724. Looking at daily totals, the 2,472 bookings recorded as early as 30th July remained a record until 21st August when 2,510 booked. Thursday, 29th August was the best day of the summer, with 2,750 bookings; this day was comparatively free of pre-booked parties and the 12 trains coped with the crowds much more easily than on many other days. At the other end of the scale, the wettest day in August Monday, 19th—provided 902 bookings. (For the uninitiated, we should mention that the daily bookings figure indicates the number of tickets sold on the Railway, while the weekly passenger journey figure counts two journeys for a return and one for a single ticket.)

On a typical peak day, each locomotive and coach clocked between 50 and 100 miles (40% up on 1967), Stationmaster Tan-y-Bwlch walked 6 miles, Control answered 200 telephone calls, Lottie Edwards opened her gates 28 times, at least one pre-booked coach party missed the train that carried its reserved seats, and at least half a dozen of the operating staff missed their evening meal.

1969

NEWS FROM THE LINE - Winter 1969

Traffic

The last official passenger train of the 1968 season ran the 19-mile return trip on Sunday 3rd November, although passengers were gladly accepted on some trial runs from Minffordd later in the month. The standard six-coach corridor-connected train set has been used continuously, often with added coaches, since a mammoth evening shunt concluded the peak, three-train service on 8th September. With refreshment service, from two buffet cars, to all 30 first-class and 137 third-class seats, an observation car, Pullman comfort for other first-class passengers, and toilet facilities, this off-season train must surely rank with the world's best on the narrow gauge.

This standard of comfort was probably appreciated most during the last fortnight in September, when the Railway was host once again to the Army, this time represented by the 65 Railway Squadron, the Army's only Railway Reserve Unit, on annual camp. With the entire stud of locomotives suffering from end-of-season temperament and more poor coal, it was understandable that the army crews took time to get used to their charges, and as a result some passengers spent a little more time on the trains than they might otherwise have done. The public had the advantage of an augmented service, with on some days four or five return trips instead of the advertised two. Specials were also provided for visiting "top brass", and one of these "crossed" a passenger train at Dduallt—the first occasion, probably in the history of the Railway, that two trains of passenger stock have been at Dduallt together.

With a few returns still to come from tours operators, it is not yet possible to give a final passenger journey figure for the season, but it promises to be in the region of 294,000, an increase of 33 per cent over 1967. Traffic receipts show an increase in the region of 59 per cent and sales receipts around 64 per cent.

Boston Lodge

The decision of the F.R. Company Board to devote a major proportion of the increased 1968 receipts to the badly-needed improvements to the locomotive stock has met with widespread approval, but nowhere more so than at Boston Lodge. The amount of work in hand will necessitate ruthless concentration on locomotive work, to the exclusion of many other matters, if the requirements of the 1969 season are to be fully met. It would seem appropriate, therefore, to provide here a review of the fleet.

Earl of Merioneth. This Fairlie only requires routine maintenance work this winter, and will be ready for heavy duties throughout the 1969 season. During the autumn some experiments were carried out with new types of flexible steam pipes, for both saturated and superheated steam, with generally favourable results. On arrival at Boston Lodge, *Earl*'s new boiler will be stored until heavy overhaul becomes necessary; in view of the age of the present boiler, a reserve at hand is a welcome insurance in the event of trouble.

Merddin Emrys. Contrary to earlier suggestions, *Merddin* is being rebuilt as a complete unit without recourse to *Earl*'s bogies. The boiler is scheduled for delivery early in the Spring of 1969 and everything possible will be done to have the locomotive available for service in the peak season. The bogies are being sent to Hunslet's, where new cylinders are to be fitted. Although improved motion with piston valves would be desirable to go with the super-heater equipment, it is felt that the tremendous amount of work involved would keep the engine in shops far too long under present circumstances. Nevertheless, "Super-Fairlie" has become firmly established in Boston Lodge vocabulary.

Blanche. After routine work this Hunslet should be ready for a lion's share of the medium duty work in 1969.

Linda. The boiler was despatched to Hunslet's on the F.R. lorry on 3rd November, and will be returning complete with superheater and new firebox early in 1969. Her reassembly is to have top priority, with a view to having her running as early in the season as possible.

Prince. The veteran was dismantled in November and the boiler prepared for inspection. In view of *Prince*'s limited capabilities with present-day traffic it is obviously essential that the more powerful engines should receive priority. However, depending of course on the extent of the boiler work required, it is hoped to find some capacity in the erecting shop for *Prince*'s rebuild during the year.

Mountaineer. Mid-October saw the Alco-Cooke 2-6-2T in service, but with very temporary weather-sheeting pending winter work on the cab and other refinements. Several trips have been made with six coaches and one test train with eight, whilst a six-coach set is being kept at Minffordd for further trial runs. The main problem has been maintaining steam pressure, but at the end of November this seemed to have been almost overcome, one of the changes being a larger chimney—experimentally she is running with *Linda*'s. On the Festiniog Convention Special on 2nd November some adhesion difficulties were experienced on a greasy rail, but with efficient sanding gear this is not expected to be a recurring problem with moderate loads. Obviously, until *Linda* returns to traffic, *Mountaineer* is going to have a very busy start to the 1969 season, and her ability to cope with a variety of duties is going to be of great importance.

The Garratt. As already mentioned, work is scheduled to start during 1969-70.

The Peckett. The ex-Harrogate Gas Works engine is scheduled in the programme after the Garratt.

Welsh Pony and *Princess*. Both are officially awaiting rebuilding, but it must be recognised that the Company's policy for the early 1970s must be to:

(a) Have the heavy-duty engines—the two Fairlies and the Garratt—in top condition

(b) Support them with an economical stud of medium-duty engines—*Blanche*, *Linda* and *Mountaineer*, together, ultimately, with the Peckett

(c) Keep *Prince* in service for light work, mainly for sentimental and prestige reasons. Possibly when very heavy boiler renewal becomes due it might be more useful to spend the money on *Welsh Pony*. The usefulness of the smaller F.R. engines is dwindling, but they have sentimental attraction and will certainly be kept running as much as possible.

We must not overlook the much maligned but invaluable diesels, which have to be maintained just as much as the more popular steam engines. *Moelwyn* and *Upnor Castle* are both available for P.W. duties, works shunting etc. The Simplex is having a long overdue and much needed overhaul of wheels and axleboxes as well as an engine exchange. Further work on *Tyke*'s engine change awaits appropriately skilled help. *Alistair* is leading an extremely active life in the Tan-y-Bwlch area, whilst the P.W. Dept.'s Wickham petrol trolley is also in active use again.

Permanent Way

The summer ended, as it began, with the accent on routine maintenance, but with some preparations being put in hand for the autumn and winter programme. Mid-September saw the P.W. gang working with army plate-layers, relaying the coal road at Minffordd exchange sidings and putting down useful amounts of top ballast near Hafod-y-Llyn and above Garnedd. The ballasting was continued in October, while sleepers were being prepared and rails sorted for the Cob relaying.

The working scene then changed to Blaenau Ffestiniog for a job which had been arranged to coincide with the Hansag working week. With a week-end boost from other Group parties, the target of lifting all metal track materials east of the old Central (G.W.) station was achieved during the week, in spite of weather hostile even by Blaenau standards. The most worthwhile materials retrieved were chairs, switches and crossings from about ten sets of points, replenishing stocks which have dwindled almost to nothing. Good numbers of "square" chairs will also be re-used in due course, but other chairs and an estimated eight tons of rail were good only for scrap and are being disposed of as such. The usable items were brought to Minffordd on the firm's lorry, which was at the P.W. Dept.'s disposal for the week. The main object of the exercise was to enable the land alongside the old Duffws station to be made available for Council use, as with the closure of the quarry inclines the Railway has no use for the old trackbed east of the Central site.

Winter on the P.W. really started on 4th November, immediately the Festiniog Convention week-end had closed the operating season—at least as far as Portmadoc was concerned—and work started on stage 2 of the long-term plan for improvements to Harbour Station track layout. Two sets of siding points were relaid in new positions, and a third point, built up from some basic components brought down from Blaenau, laid in. The net results are an increase in the effective length of No. 2 road (on which the "B" train is usually stabled in summer), a considerable extension to No. 4 road (carriage siding), which is being lengthened to end alongside the coaling stage, and a turnout which can be extended into two more sidings on the seaward side at a future date.

On 16th November lifting of track on the Cob was commenced and the long-awaited relaying began in earnest, helped by excellent Group working parties at week-ends. Bull-head rail ex-Penrhyn Quarry Railway is being used at the Portmadoc end, whilst the bull-head rail already *in situ* at the Boston Lodge end will require resleepering and fishplate adjustment. The ex-W.H.R. flat-bottom rail in the centre of the Cob is being re-used, (but with sole-plates, clips and standard screws), to keep keying-up and maintenance to a minimum at this very exposed location.

1969 Timetable

The provisional timetable for 1969 shows a further extension of the operating season. At the start of the season trains will leave Portmadoc at 11.00 and 14.30 on Saturdays and Sundays 15th, 16th, 22nd, 23rd March, then daily from the 29th March until 16th May, when the service begins to build up. Twelve trains daily are shown for weekdays in the peak season, with train crossings varying between Minffordd and Penrhyn in an irregular but carefully thought-out way. This peak service will also operate during Spring Bank Holiday week.

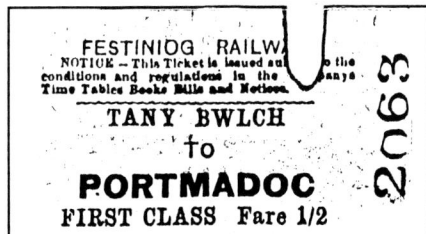

FESTINIOG RAILWAY
NOTICE — This Ticket is issued and to the conditions and regulations in the Company's Time Tables Books Bills and Notices.

TANY BWLCH
to
PORTMADOC
FIRST CLASS Fare 1/2

2063

110. The Deviation had gained good momentum by 1969. This is Barn site in January, viewed through the scaffolding of Rhoslyn Bridge which would eventually be the key part of the spiral line. The dig is on the right and the fill is in the centre. (A.G.W.Garraway)

111. Rhoslyn Bridge was to be supported by four concrete columns cast in place. A tipper wagon containing concrete is at the bottom of the picture. In the middle is a suspended wheelbarrow loaded with the same. The man near the pulley is ready to tip the contents into the formwork. (A.G.W.Garraway)

NEWS FROM THE LINE - Spring 1969

Locomotive mileages recorded during 1968 were as follows:

Locomotive		1968	Total under Present Administration
Prince ..	..	3,806	40,287
Earl of Merioneth	..	5,697	29,859
Merddin Emrys	..	nil	11,924
Linda ..	..	4,330	24,378
Blanche	..	5,823	14,881
Mountaineer ..	..	252	300
Moelwyn	..	1,301	18,550
Upnor Castle ..	..	195	195
Tyke ..	..	nil	180
Alistair	..	825	825
Simplex Tractor	..	1,281	4,939
Wickham Trolley	..	917	8,413

The total of 24,427 locomotive miles compares with 19,033 in 1967 and shows that the increase in passenger traffic was not lightly won.

The coaching stock mileages also show substantial increases. Nos. 14, 100, 104 and 105 head the list, each being over the 10,000 miles mark. Bow-sider No. 20 covered over 7,000—an exceptionally high figure for one of the old F.R. bogies—and at the other end of the scale the four-wheelers were not many miles short of 2,500 apiece. Total carriage mileage was 123,002, as against 78,441 in 1967.

Boston Lodge

With up to five steam locomotives being worked on, almost simultaneously, throughout the winter, it is too early to expect concrete results in terms of gleaming engines in "ex works" condition. Even *Blanche*'s "minor routine"

work has consumed many man-days, and progress on other locomotives has met unforeseen snags. However, *Mountaineer*'s cab is taking shape, and *Linda*'s frame assembly is being prepared for the return of the boiler from Hunslet's. A pony truck is to be added to give greater stability to the engine. One of the inside-journaled axles from the bogie ex *Moel Tryfan* is to be used for this truck, whilst the other will be retained for future use with *Blanche*. The addition will be arranged so as not to affect the adhesion weight of these locomotives.

The ever-growing fleet of coaches has, of course, required the usual winter examination and maintenance of running gear, which in some cases has proved quite extensive, due, no doubt, to the greatly increased mileages. Assembly of the new observation car, No. 101, is well advanced, but has been awaiting the next visit of the specialist volunteers responsible for such work. The interior of the iron-framed bogie coach No. 16 is beginning to reflect the many years of painstaking care put into its restoration; the historic three-seat first-class coupé compartment holds particular promise, with lavishly inlaid panels, ex-Pullman car *Eunice*, expertly reduced to narrow-gauge dimensions. A fair amount of work remains to be done, particularly on the running gear.

An important aspect of rolling stock policy not previously recorded in the *Magazine* has been the adoption of unlined cherry red livery for the old coaches. The shade is very similar to the basic pre-war livery (ignoring the rainbow hues of the "Toy Railway" era), but without the time-consuming lining out. The colour was chosen mainly for its hard-wearing qualities, but it is also hoped that it will blend with the varnished livery when trains are composed of old and new coaches. So far, coaches Nos. 11, 12, 15, 16 and 22 have been or are being so painted, together with brake vans Nos. 1 and 2, whilst bow-sider No. 19 will be next on the list. Some of the painting has been done by compressed air spraying, by the members of the East Anglian Group responsible for the superlative finish on No. 9 van.

112. With the increased use, Tan-y-bwlch water tank was sometimes exhausted, so a new tank was put up, a pile of sleepers supporting the former road vehicle body. (A.G.W.Garraway)

113. As part of the FR publicity for getting back to Blaenau, *Princess* was transported by road and put on display there on 18th June. The site was outside the Queens Hotel. The stone pillar on the left was part of the approach to the bridge over the former FR line to Duffws. (A.G.W.Garraway)

114. For the Prince of Wales' Investiture in July *Earl of Merioneth* (one of the Duke of Edinburgh's titles) carried a headboard. Figures showed the FR to be the second most popular visitor location in one year. As in Investiture Year, Caernarfon Castle was at the top. (A.G.W.Garraway)

115. The Alco was photographed in July after being given a cab to the FR loading gauge, the name *Mountaineer* and the bell from the old FR engine of that name. It still carried its 1917 boiler, which had been retubed in 1968. (A.G.W.Garraway)

NEWS FROM THE LINE - Summer 1969

Traffic

In contrast to the start of the 1968 season, this year's traffic has given us little to write about so far. The figures are satisfactory enough, with Easter week numbers being a record for that week but only to the extent of five passenger journeys. With the boost of daily trains early in May, when previously they have only run on selected days, the gap has widened since Easter, and all things considered the prospects are quite bright for the summer.

Easter was notable mainly for the exceptionally dry and windy weather, with fire prevention as the main job for volunteers, but the Monday also brought the first of three ceremonies which took place within four weeks. A special train was run from Portmadoc to Minffordd to commemorate the centenary of the introduction of articulated locomotives on the F.R. *Earl of Merioneth*, flag bedecked and in spotless condition, hauled the train, on which a group of local ladies in period costume were the Company's guests.

On A.G.M. afternoon, in very different weather conditions, John Ransom formally named *Mountaineer* in a short ceremony at Dduallt. In addition to the nameplates, this locomotive carries the bell from the original No. 3 *Mountaineer* which, together with a chime whistle from the N.C.B., Philadelphia, gives an appropriately realistic American atmosphere when running at speed. *Mountaineer* was in charge on the evening of 8th May, when Will and Bessie Jones joined Mr. Pegler and a 100% turn-out of permanent staff, wives and friends on the occasion of their Ruby Wedding; there was additional cause for celebration when it was learnt that the Dukes family had been increased by the arrival of a son. Under Arwyn Morgan's guidance the Festiniog male voice choir was going well by the time the special arrived back at Portmadoc.

Easter Saturday saw the first outing of the all-red "B" train, and its appearance seemed to meet with general approval, as it did again on A.G.M. day. Its buffet car was attached to the main train during A.G.M. evening, to give extra service on the late night special; as a social occasion the excursion seems to have been a great success and accepted as a substitute for the traditional gathering at Minffordd prior to departure of the return BR special.

Spring Bank Holiday Week

Week-end traffic on the roads across the Cob and through Penrhyn seemed heavier than ever before, with a half-mile queue through Minffordd after midnight on the Friday night, but the trains were rarely more than comfortably full, with figures akin to last year's. The three-train service got off to a shaky start on the Monday, with both *Blanche* and *Mountaineer* suffering from minor ailments, and with the timetable demanding top level performances from all three available steam engines it was found desirable to pilot *Mountaineer* with *Moelwyn* for most of the week. Timekeeping steadily improved as all concerned got used to the routine, but the strain of maintaining such an intensive service with three engines brought back memories of the 1962 locomotive crisis. In that year *Linda's* arrival eased the situation, and it is to be hoped that her re-entry into service following overhaul will have the same effect this year in time for the peak service.

At the end of Spring Bank Holiday week, total traffic figures for the season were virtually identical to those at the end of the 1968 bank holiday week, which was a week later. The actual passenger journey figure for the week was 21,592, as compared with 19,870 in 1968. These satisfactory results were only made possible by the sterling efforts of the Boston Lodge staff, who worked very long hours, including two overnight sessions, to keep the motive power mobile.

Boston Lodge

Although handling a good share of the early-season traffic, *Mountaineer* was still receiving attention during May. The cab needed finishing off and other front-end adjustments made. Her disinclination to steam freely with anything more than a modest load has been a matter for some concern, but the indications during May were that the difficulties were definitely being overcome.

Linda's boiler arrived back from Hunslet Engine Co. at the end of April, complete with new firebox and superheater.

Observation car 100 and buffet car 14 have both been in the shops for minor repairs and modification, the effect of the latter being to provide accommodation for the guard in 100 and leave the business end of 14 completely free for much-needed kitchen use. Bow-sider No. 19 was the fifth bogie coach to emerge from the paint shop in red livery. During May Nos. 16 and 101 were side-by-side in the erecting shop and various opinions were being offered as to which would enter traffic first and when.

Essential work has taken members of the works staff away from the "Lodge", one particular assignment involving water tanks up the line. On 12th May the two tanks at Tan-y-Bwlch were taken down and replaced by a 3,500-gallon five-compartment tank from a scrapped road tanker. This was quite a major operation, involving the hire of a ten-ton crane for the day, and was done without interruption of the train service. In order to provide an alternative water supply while the plumbing of the new tank was being installed, Dduallt tank was restored to working order, and it was *Blanche* who had the privilege of taking the first fill on the afternoon of the 13th.

A welcome addition to the miscellaneous vehicle fleet was the set of bolster wagons returned from the East Anglian Group on A.G.M. day, embodying some first-class timber work. Their main use will be the transporting of telegraph poles, but when the S. & T. Dept. are not around the P.W. men will do their best to see that the bolsters do not lie idle for too long.

Permanent Way

By the end of March, the transformation of the Cob from the worst to the best stretch of track below Dduallt was completed. It is now all bull-head from the king points at Portmadoc to alongside the carriage shed at Boston Lodge, apart from a good stretch of ex-W.H.R. flat bottom rail in the middle of the Cob. Some of the bull-head rail at the Boston Lodge end is rather worn by normal bull-head standards due to wheelslip burn during its first spell of duty in Moelwyn tunnel, and defied efforts to set it really straight and true, but it nevertheless rides smoothly enough.

With the Cob finished, Portmadoc sidings received some rather hasty treatment. No. 2 road was lifted over six inches for several lengths and is now at roughly the same level as roads 1 and 3, improving the appearance of the layout and assisting coach oiling. A variety of work locations then followed. Some alterations were made to trackwork at the bottom end of Tan-y-Bwlch station, to enable the abutments of the footbridge to be concreted in their correct positions, then at Easter work started on the relaying of Penrhyn loop. Good progress was made with the digging out in spite of depletion of the labour force to form fire patrols, and the lifting and relaying followed on subsequent week-ends. The trap point was completed in time for Spring Bank Holiday and the headshunt finished a couple of days later.

Immediately after Easter the maintenance specialists—Fred Howes and John Babbage—began their summer stint of lifting joints, changing poor sleepers and doing general length maintenance, while Ron Lester, Norman Gurley and Rodney Smith (who call themselves the "construction" gang when not on straightforward maintenance) took in hand the necessary improvements to Dduallt station. These included the building up of the platform with quarry debris and a top layer of granite dust, the realignment and packing of the loop, and the provision of seats, noticeboards and other products from Group workshops. Meanwhile, members of the fencing gang attacked the trees felled by the deviationists, splitting them into several hundred fence stakes; these formed return loads to Minffordd for some of the wagons used to take quarry debris and granite dust to Dduallt and helped to provide some useful extra weight for the inevitable gravity trains.

The permanent way depot at Minffordd has gradually been taking on a new look in recent months. The stocks of usable bull-head rails and chairs ex Penrhyn Quarry Railway have been considerably reduced; good stocks of square double-head chairs are now evident and useful sums have been raised by disposal of worn double-head rail, "S" chairs etc. Some 1,500 pairs of fishplates have been purchased new, to replace badly rusted Penrhyn and old F.R. bull-head plates. (Using fishplates that actually *fish* will be a real novelty!) On 16th May came perhaps the most notable development of all, in the form of two BR wagons containing 1,000 yards of good quality 75 lb. per yard flat bottom rail from some recently lifted sidings in the Cardiff area.

With stocks and sources of F.R.-size chaired track virtually eliminated, flat bottom track is an inevitable part of the Railway's future, and further sources of suitable rail are being considered.

Staff News

After seven years at Boston Lodge, first as an apprentice and then as fitter/driver, David Baskcomb departed at the end of April to sample the very different working conditions at Trawsfynydd Atomic Power Station. We wish him well in his new post and are sure that he will not vanish completely from the F.R. scene.

There are several new arrivals to report, though most can hardly be described as newcomers. After many years as Senior Guard, Alan Heywood has finally succumbed to the inevitable, and has given up his teaching career to join the Railway as Traffic Manager. He and his wife, Pam, expect to be taking up permanent residence in Penrhyn about the time this *Magazine* is due to be published and we extend to them the warmest of welcomes.

Also at Harbour Station, Bob Smallman has become firmly established behind the "Railwayana" counter, complete with some new ideas and heraldic shields, although at time of writing he is deputising for Nick Knight who is off sick and unable to supervise the operation of the buffet cars.

At Boston Lodge, Morris Davies joined the staff at the beginning of June to restore the fitting strength and, incidentally, help swell the Welsh speaking element. Morris came to us from Minffordd Quarry, and it can only be hoped that our future supplies of ballast will not be delayed by increasing plant breakdowns. He has had experience at sea and with various engineering firms, which should be an asset with our diverse plant and equipment.

There is one newcomer in the permanent way gang, Rodney Smith—a regular Hansag volunteer—having filled the gap created by Bill Evans' expected co-option to traffic duties for the summer.

Finally, whilst on the subject of new arrivals, we congratulate Paul and Ann Dukes, and Bob and Christine Harris, on the occasion of recent additions to their families.

Our best wishes for a speedy recovery go to Helen Goldstraw, daughter of *Mountaineer*-driver Roy and caterer Kay, who was injured in a road accident early in June.

Nature Trail

On Sunday 18th May, The Press, TV and various dignitaries assembled at Tan-y-Bwlch for the opening of Coed Llyn Mair Nature Trail. This will provide visitors to the area with educational *divertissement* and help them to work up a healthy thirst before visiting the station café. The trail is about one mile long, and normally takes about an hour to complete, the alternative starting points being by the entrance to Tan-y-Bwlch station car park and by a new car park on the road near Llyn Mair.

The Nature Conservancy have prepared an illustrated leaflet to guide the visitor round the trail, describing the flora, fauna and geographical features, and also giving some useful information on the history of the Tan-y-Bwlch Estate. The leaflets are priced at 6d. each and may be purchased at Portmadoc station and Tan-y-Bwlch café. John Harrison, Tan-y-Bwlch Station, Maentwrog, Blaenau Ffestiniog, Merioneth, will be pleased to send a copy by post on receipt of foolscap stamped addressed envelope and an additional 6d. stamp.

116. To assist with the transfer of materials and equipment from road to rail, a gantry crane was constructed in Minffordd Yard. The goods shed (left) houses the well equipped PW workshop. (A.G.W.Garraway)

117. Originally there had been access to Boston Lodge through an arch leading off the road on the curve; the arch is still visible. During WWI, when the works had been used for munitions manufacture, lavatories had been created in the underground passage by blanking off the archway. In 1969 smells and general drain problems indicated that all was not well. Extensive excavations showed that the drains consisted, in part, of a slate trough about 5ft underground, the lid of which had collapsed and/or had been blocked with ashes etc. In view of uncertainties regarding the drainage system, the hole that had been created was shored up rather than refilled so that access could be obtained again. (A.G.W.Garraway)

NEWS FROM THE LINE - Autumn 1969

Traffic

Investiture year has been one of fluctuating fortunes for the Railway. The end of Spring Bank Holiday week saw passenger journey figures 8,500 up on 1968, representing an increase of 17%, but during the following two months the percentage was steadily whittled down until by 26th July the increase was only 7,700. Several weeks had shown reductions from 1968, that of the last in June by 1,400, and investiture week itself did not bring very exciting figures. It was the last three weeks of the full summer service that really brought the boost everyone had been waiting for; early in September the 1968 totals had been left behind and the forecasters were busy estimating by how much the modest target of 300,000 journeys would be exceeded. The increase had been pushed up to nearly 18,000 with passenger receipts 17% up and sales receipts 25% up.

This was a much rosier picture than had seemed possible at the end of July. Not only were traffic figures disappointing at that time, but things were running far from smoothly due to locomotive problems more serious than at any time in recent history.

From 11th July, when *Earl of Merioneth* was taken into shops for essential repairs, until 6th August, when the Fairlie worked the evening train as a trial run, there were only two steam engines available. Even in ideal circumstances, *Blanche* and *Mountaineer* could not be expected to work several trains daily from Portmadoc to Dduallt sharing all available rolling stock—and more often than not traffic density demanded that all rolling stock was used. Thus on Sunday 13th July, at the start of the last week of the "Spring" service, *Upnor Castle* hauled a test train to Dduallt satisfactorily and two diesel-hauled relief trains were added to the timetable, leaving Portmadoc at 13.20 and 15.30. One of these on the Tuesday had an unscheduled stop at Rhiw Goch when *Upnor Castle* burst a radiator hose, and *Mountaineer* was despatched from Tan-y-Bwlch to haul up the failed diesel and train in a brief moment of glory. A new hose had been brought up to Tan-y-Bwlch by car and *Upnor Castle* soon resumed its journey.

Next day came the first of five consecutive visits from some very unpleasant Wednesdays-only gremlins. On this occasion they removed a pin from inside *Blanche*'s dome while she was waiting to leave Portmadoc with the first train of the day, and nothing happened when the driver opened the regulator. *Mountaineer* worked the train, *Upnor Castle* took *Blanche* to the works then worked the 11.30, *Mountaineer* took the 13.20 relief and then *Upnor Castle* failed with a hot box at Penrhyn on the 14.00 Fortunately *Blanche* had by then been repaired and was able to go to Penrhyn to take over.

With the start of the Summer service the following week-end it was intended to use *Upnor Castle* on the third diagram, but on her first trip she ran hot again and for a while there was no alternative but to use the faithful *Moelwyn*. Her train consisted of an ex-Welsh Highland coach and Buffet Car 14, with, after a coupling modification, No. 2 van for the guard. There was always a good head of steam in the radiator on the up journey, but with a steady supply of hot water from the buffet car *Moelwyn* performed unfailingly, earning an estimated £1,000 in fares. *Upnor Castle*'s appearances were spasmodic, but by taking larger trains she, too, earned the best part of £1,000.

A week later a misunderstanding at Penrhyn resulted in a one-bogie derailment on the top points. It was fortunately a very minor matter in the sense that the only damage was a sheered cotter pin on the point blades, but it resulted in one peak train being lost and in important lessons being learnt. The following Wednesday 6th August, *Upnor Castle* was doing one of its intermittent spells of duty when it failed completely at Dduallt (more usually its failures enabled it to limp back to Portmadoc with its train), and after a delay the result was a steam-hauled down train of ten bogies and six four-wheelers.

Needless to say, the reappearance of *Earl of Merioneth* that same evening was heralded with great rejoicing; in fact, to ensure that everyone could celebrate the occasion a relief was run to the evening train next day, it having been the first day of the peak season that all trains had run to time. The diesels had saved the day as far as passenger figures—and receipts—were concerned, but their use on passenger trains is not intended to be part of the F.R.'s image. Throughout the period of their regular use, passengers had been kept informed, both by noticeboards and public address announcements, of which trains were expected to be diesel-hauled, and they always had the opportunity of waiting for a steam-hauled train if they wished. Few did.

The gremlins hadn't quite finished. On Wednesday 13th *Earl* had to be kept in for the day, but by this time *Upnor Castle*'s driving axle bearings had been whitemetalled and she completed all three trips of the C diagram in fine style. The gremlins retired in disorder, not to return during August.

Throughout the rest of the peak season the service ran very smoothly. The engines had to work hard, of course, with the short turn-rounds a continual headache, but with two crews rostered for each nobody had to work excessive hours on the footplate. *Blanche* and *Mountaineer* had done all that could be expected of them during the weeks of crisis, the former making up for the inadequacies of the diesels by taking nine bogies on occasions and the latter, whilst more restricted in loads and consuming prodigious amounts of fuel, proving both reliable and spritely. Variations in the quality of coal supplies called for careful firing, especially on *Mountaineer*.

It will be recalled that in 1968 *Blanche* headed the mileage table with 5,823 miles. This year she passed the 8,000 mark before the end of the summer service.

Finally, a few more passenger statistics for those who like them: the journeys made in the seven weeks of the summer service were respectively 16,869, 23,036, 22,718, 22,928, 25,603, 25,902 and 19,952, totalling 157,008. The 1968 best was 23,976. Although 2,400 bookings for a day was exceeded seven times, as compared with three times in 1968, the record for a day was not broken. Probably the most satisfactory aspect of the season's figures was the increased patronage of the evening trains, due mainly, no doubt, to the introduction of cheap evening fares. The 17.25 train averaged 98 bookings and the 19.00 106 bookings, as compared with 44 on the 17.45 and 58 on the 19.45 in 1968, and the introduction of the 19.00 on Saturdays and, especially, Sundays proved a well worth-while innovation.

Traffic remained good throughout September. A relief train was run at 13.20 from 15th to 18th, and during week commencing 22nd an experimental service was introduced with departures at 11.00, 13.00 and 15.00 from Portmadoc and 12.00, 14.00 and 16.00 from Dduallt. Although not shown on the timetable, the 13.00/13.20 train was well patronised and helped to avoid excessively heavy loadings on the main afternoon service.

Boston Lodge

The basic problem with *Mountaineer*'s steam pipes was overcome by fitting completely new, external pipes from the boiler to the steam chests and blanking off the cavity through the cylinder/saddle casting. This latter operation continued to give some trouble, however, and it was eventually cured by filling the cavity irrevocably with concrete.

Meanwhile, in late June *Earl of Merioneth* was beginning to leak badly from the crown stays in one firebox, due to failure of the ferrules. In 1962 this fault had put *Merddin Emrys* out of action for the season, but this time the necessary equipment was available and it was not thought that rectification would take very long. As soon as *Mountaineer* was pronounced fit for the rigours of peak traffic, work was started on *Earl*, but hopes of completing the job quickly were soon dashed. Unlike previous experience with *Merddin*, only nine stays allowed themselves to be screwed out; the remaining 27 had to be drilled out and the holes retapped—a slow and laborious process, especially in the confines of a small firebox in the peak of a hot summer.

Blanche and *Mountaineer* had to receive immediate attention from time to time to keep them running, and *Upnor Castle* came in almost daily for axle-box attention. The manufacturers and oil experts were consulted but even a lethal mixture of castor oil and Graphite failed to keep her running cool and in desperation the brasses of the two driving axleboxes were whitemetalled.

All this left very little skilled labour for other urgent work. Progress on *Linda* was slow but steady, dominated by the intricate yet heavy work involved in building what is virtually a new front end for the locomotive. She was obviously not going to be ready for the peak service and so the more immediate revenue-earning potentiality of coach No. 16 raised its priority, once three engines were running again. The bodywork was mounted temporarily on the set of spare N.W.N.G. bogies and the coach entered service on 30th August. The last true F.R. bogie coach to be put back into service, its restoration has been largely the dedicated work of one man, hastened in the end by permanent staff who have taken care to ensure that his high standards have not been lowered. The first-class accommodation, and especially the unique coupé compartment, surely sets an entirely new standard in rolling stock preservation.

While *Earl* was out of action the unexpected opportunity was taken of getting at the bug-boxes with paint-spraying equipment, and so during the first week in August the last vestige of green and ivory livery disappeared without trace.

Permanent Way

As usual in the summer, track maintenance has received first priority, with up to five staff and a similar number of volunteers engaged on the work in various locations. Larger parties of volunteers have been working at Minffordd Exchange Sidings, where an extensive programme of relaying and layout improvements has been started in connection with the conversion of the large slate sheds (until recently occupied by Davies Bros.) for carriage storage.

Thought has already been given to the winter's programme, of which the major part will be located between Minffordd and Penrhyn. The full length of Gwyndy Bank and the cutting above is to be relaid, mainly with the 75 lbs./yd. flat bottom rail from Barry, long welded on the straights. In the same area, the Council are widening the road under Nazareth Chapel bridge, and in conjunction with this the F.R. are putting in a new deck to replace the present slate slabs. Towards the end of the winter the top end of Dduallt station is to be realigned to put the top end of the main line and the loop on to the deviation embankment; this will permit the laying of semi-permanent track on the spiral later in the year, which in turn will facilitate the completion of Rhoslyn Bridge.

There should be plenty of work for all comers throughout the winter, and as usual at this time of year the P.W. gang invite volunteers to join them for a week or more in the autumn, when a late holiday can be very rewarding.

S. & T.

An important job completed just in time for the summer service was the installation of "short-section" electric train staff control on the Minffordd-Penrhyn and Penrhyn-Tan-y-Bwlch sections. When Penrhyn is manned and trains require to cross there, short-section working is introduced; at other times the long-section Minffordd-Tan-y-Bwlch system is used. Paradoxically, the short sections use full-size staffs and the long one miniatures. Needless to say, there is a safeguard to ensure that the long-section staff cannot be drawn while short-section working is in operation, and vice versa; this consists of a chain tying one each of the short-section staffs to a key at Penrhyn. The key switches on the long-section staff circuit and the short-section staff instruments are too far away from the switch box for the chain to reach them. All three stations have to co-operate to release the key. Changeover is a lugubrious affair analogous to a manacled prisoner changing his underpants.

(Railway Magazine October 1969)

118. The new boiler for *Merddin Emrys* arrived by road at Minffordd on 9th October and is being loaded on its side onto wagons for transfer to Boston Lodge. Note that there are two separate fireboxes with a common water space. (A.G.W.Garraway)

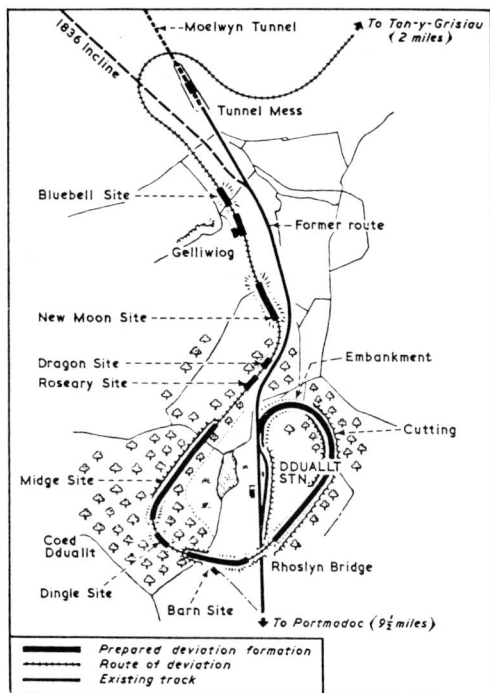

Map labels:
- To Tan-y-Grisiau (2 miles)
- Moelwyn Tunnel
- 1836 Incline
- Tunnel Mess
- Bluebell Site
- Former route
- Gelliwiog
- New Moon Site
- Embankment
- Dragon Site
- Roseary Site
- Cutting
- Midge Site
- DDUALLT STN.
- Coed Dduallt
- Dingle Site
- Rhoslyn Bridge
- Barn Site
- To Portmodoc (9½ miles)
- Prepared deviation formation
- Route of deviation
- Existing track

119. By 1969, pairs of rails were being welded together electrically at Boston Lodge. On the right is the shed seen unclad in picture no. 94 and on the left is the now demolished Long Shed. (A.G.W.Garraway)

120. A number of smaller bridges and culverts consisted of slate slabs and over the years these had disintegrated. A new concrete span had to be put in at Capel Nazareth, below Penrhyn. The photograph was taken in the last weeks of the decade and typifies the hidden problems of taking over a railway having an infrastructure intended for a horse-worked tramway. (A.G.W.Garraway)